# LUPUS: THE BODY
# AGAINST ITSELF

Also by Sheldon Paul Blau, M.D., and Dodi Schultz

*ARTHRITIS: Complete, Up-to-Date Facts for Patients and Their Families*

Other Books on Health and Medicine Co-authored by Dodi Schultz

*THE FIRST FIVE YEARS* (with Virginia E. Pomeranz, M.D.)

*FROM 1 TO 2: YOUR BABY'S SECOND YEAR* (with Virginia E. Pomeranz, M.D.)

*WE WANT TO HAVE A BABY* (with James T. Howard, Jr., M.D.)

*THE MOTHERS' AND FATHERS' MEDICAL ENCYCLO-PEDIA* (with Virginia E. Pomeranz, M.D.)

*HOME AND FAMILY MEDICAL EMERGENCIES* (with Seth F. Abramson, M.D.)

*THE HEADACHE BOOK* (with Arnold P. Friedman, M.D., and Shervert H. Frazier, Jr., M.D.)

# LUPUS: THE BODY AGAINST ITSELF

COMPLETELY UPDATED AND
REVISED EDITION

*Sheldon Paul Blau, M.D.*
*and Dodi Schultz*

DOUBLEDAY & COMPANY, INC.
GARDEN CITY, NEW YORK
1984

*Library of Congress Cataloging in Publication Data*
Library of Congress Catalog Card Number 82–45962

Blau, Sheldon Paul.
Lupus: the body against itself.
Includes index
1. Lupus erythematosus, Systemic. I. Schultz, Dodi.
II. Title.
RC924.5.L85B56   1984        616.9′78
ISBN 0-385-18800-5

*To the patients,*
*with hope,*
*and to*
*Bette and Ed,*
*with love*

# CONTENTS

# PART ONE: THE PUZZLE

At the beginning of the first edition of this book, we stressed
—with a certain amount of incredulity and perhaps indigna-
tion—the lack of space and attention devoted by the lay
media to lupus. Lupus afflicts, as we pointed out, at least half
a million and probably close to a million Americans; most of
those it strikes are young women. The systemic form of lupus, with which this book is concerned, is, we emphasized,
diagnosed only with great difficulty—suggesting that many
cases of this potentially extremely serious disorder remained
undiagnosed and untreated, or *mis*diagnosed and hence *mis*-
treated.

It is gratifying to report that lupus is no longer neglected.
Popular media ranging from *American Health* and the New
York *Times* to *Family Circle* have made lupus, if not precisely
a household word, at least an entity not entirely foreign to
the public. At the same time, heightened activity on the
research front has made the other news media far more
aware of lupus and they, too, have helped to bring the topic
to public attention.

Probably cases of lupus still remain undiagnosed and untreated. Probably lupus is in many instances still mistaken for
some other illness. And now, with that increased awareness,
probably many cases of *other* disorders and diseases are mistaken for lupus.

Part of the increasing awareness has stemmed from the
growing focus on the body's immune system, its function and
dysfunction, and the realization of the role the latter can play
in problems from infertility to the devastating acute condi-

tion known as acquired immune deficiency syndrome (AIDS). In a sense, lupus is the obverse of the AIDS coin. In AIDS, the system seems—for reasons unknown at this writing—to lurch to a halt, abandoning the body's defenses and leaving it vulnerable to assault by alien invaders causing seldom-seen diseases.

In lupus, on the other hand, as we shall see, the body's defenders do not sink into nodding lethargy but rather are stirred to inappropriate activity, striking out wildly not against foreign incursions but against the very organism of which they are a part. Why this happens remains a mystery, as it was seven years ago when the first edition of this book was published. Still, in those seven years, new clues have emerged—no longer the totally random clues of the seventies but hinting, now, of causal patterns and, hopefully, solutions.

A major step in the solution of any quandary is concise definition of the problem. Medically, that means clear description and diagnosis—including differentiation of the disease from others. Over the years, great strides have been made in clarifying the condition called lupus. And although the picture has still not been brought into perfect focus, it is nevertheless far sharper than it was just a decade ago.

# 1. Naming the Nemesis

Many centuries ago, Hippocrates described a disease that frightened physicians and victims alike. He characterized it as an erosive, disfiguring malady, eating away at the skin and flesh of the face. We don't know what ill—or, more likely, ills —he was picturing. But in the mid-nineteenth century a number of writers bestowed the name "lupus" (Latin for "wolf") upon what they thought he had described: an affliction causing the sort of damage that might result from the bite of a ravenous wolf. They, too, were probably denoting a number of different diseases.

Foremost among them was one that came to be called *lupus vulgaris;* it is now known, much more accurately, as cutaneous tuberculosis, and it no longer causes the tissue devastation it once did, for the same reason that other kinds of tuberculosis are no longer the threats they once were: the cause of tuberculosis, whatever the parts of the body it attacks, is known, and there are medications that deal effectively with *Mycobacterium tuberculosis,* the tuberculosis bacillus.

By the 1840s, a salient characteristic of the lupus rash had been noted and described by Ferdinand von Hebra of Vienna as occurring "mainly on the face, on the cheeks and nose in a distribution not dissimilar to a butterfly." This rash (which does not always appear in lupus) has since been known to physicians and patients alike as "the butterfly rash." It was the Frenchman Pierre Cazenave who, in 1851, introduced the term *lupus erythemateux*—lupus characterized by redness—and the Latin version has since been used internationally to refer to the disease, differentiating this noncontagious entity once and for all from other conditions, including infections, afflicting facial skin. Later, the Viennese Moritz Kaposi (yes, the physician of Kaposi's sarcoma fame) observed that fever, arthritis, and other systemic phenomena could be part of the lupus picture.

Still, it was not until the turn of the century that the distinguished Canadian physician Sir William Osler, then working and teaching at Johns Hopkins University in Baltimore, published a series of thoughtful papers concluding in no uncertain terms that lupus erythematosus was a systemic disorder, affecting various parts of the body—not only the skin, but the joints and internal organs as well, and sometimes not including cutaneous symptoms at all.

Over the next several decades a number of "new diseases" were described, only to be finally placed in the category that had come to be called "acute disseminated lupus erythematosus" and later "systemic" lupus erythematosus (SLE), distinguishing it from "discoid" lupus erythematosus (DLE), a form in which disc-shaped lesions appear on the skin and in which other parts of the body rarely, if ever, become involved. DLE is now considered probably a variant of what is a single disease—or perhaps a single *spectrum* of disease that manifests itself differently in different individuals.

Certainly the variety of manifestations is among the most striking features of lupus. That dermatologists, those medical specialists dealing with disorders of the skin, have in their texts and journals devoted much time and space to lupus is understandable. But even a cursory survey of medical literature over the past twenty or twenty-five years reveals that articles dealing with aspects of lupus have appeared in the publications of nearly every imaginable specialty, subspecialty, and branch of professional health care. Journals devoted to cardiology, hematology, psychiatry, eye-ear-nose-and-throat diseases, dentistry, respiratory disease, neurology, and gastroenterology have published lengthy and learned discussions of lupus—and so have periodicals in the fields of pediatrics and pathology, of chest disease and surgery, of allergy, pharmacology, gynecology, renal disease, and environmental health.

What *kind* of disease or disorder is lupus? In whose province does it really lie?

The interest of all those myriad specialists in lupus is legitimate. In the 1940s, lupus came to be classified, along with rheumatoid arthritis and a number of other disorders of a more or less chronic nature, as a "collagen disease." Collagen is a specific protein substance that forms an important part of connective-tissue fibrils throughout the body. Because the victims are generally adults, because these are for the most part systemic rather than localized disorders, and because there is in most instances joint inflammation, they came to be accepted as the province of internal medicine in general and of rheumatology—a subspecialty of internal medicine—in particular.

With further understanding of the nature of lupus, a second group of physicians are finding themselves equally involved. All that is connective tissue is not necessarily collagen; thus, the categorization of lupus (as well as rheumatoid arthritis) as a *connective-tissue disorder* has gained favor. And as sophisticated technology has offered more insight into what lupus is, another medical specialty is also finding it a special and absorbing challenge.

That specialty is *immunology.* Related to such generally familiar words as "immunity" and "immunization," the term suggests the study of infectious disease and the development of immunity thereto. That is indeed part of immunology's concern, but only a part. It encompasses the entire spectrum of the body's responses to provoking agents, as a class termed *antigens*—including allergens as well as infection-causing organisms such as bacteria and viruses. Such responses very frequently include inflammation of one sort or another, inflammation that is, essentially, a signal that an antigen-antibody reaction is taking place, a marshaling of the body's defenses, whether generally or locally, against the foreign intrusion.

Sometimes, when an individual has developed immunity

—as by vaccination—against a particular disease-causing antigen, there is no consciousness of the threat. Sometimes, if such a mechanism has not been developed—if, for example, an individual's upper respiratory passages are attacked by one of the more than one hundred known rhinoviruses, the organisms responsible for most cases of the common cold—the raging antigen-antibody battle and its accompanying inflammation are all too evident. Still, the conflict is relatively brief. Whether the infection lasts days, weeks, or months, the battle is at last resolved one way or the other.

Lupus is different. While it may display all the characteristics of inflammatory processes found in infections, it continues—or comes and goes at unpredictable intervals—as a chronic condition, succumbing to no known antibiotics or other anti-infection agents. Further, there is no explanation for the unrelenting attack, no identifiable infectious organism or other foreign invader. While antibodies are demonstrably active in lupus, their activity appears undirected. Or, more accurately, *mis*directed: in lupus, more dramatically than in any other connective-tissue disorder, the body appears to have marshaled its not inconsiderable defenses against its own tissues, furiously attacking and sometimes successfully destroying what are literally the fibers of its own being.

The connective-tissue disorders are also known collectively as *autoimmune disorders*—disorders manifesting self-attack, self-repulsion on the cellular level. Rheumatoid arthritis and other connective-tissue disorders can also, to an extent, be so described. But lupus is the prototype, the classic and confounding example of what is perhaps the most perplexing puzzle in medicine, not excluding the aberrant cell proliferation of the cancers: the body actively, viciously mobilized against itself.

# 2. *The Spectrum*

"Bizarre" is one appropriate adjective that has been popularly applied to lupus. Consider the following typical cases (not real people but amalgams of actual patients).

*Cathy, age fifteen.* She first went to the doctor one summer complaining of aching joints, especially those of her wrists and fingers. She also had a scaly rash on her ears. Her doctor had the justifiable feeling that she'd been through an individualistic reaction to rubella, which had been making the rounds that year and frequently causes a transient arthritis, more often in teenagers and adults than in small children. The rash seemed unrelated and, like many such rashes, cleared up with regular application of a corticosteroid ointment. But a year later the joint pains returned, along with a fairly low fever. There was also a reddening of Cathy's skin over her nose and cheeks. Cathy has systemic lupus.

*Alison, age twenty-eight.* Married and the mother of a three-year-old daughter, Alison was hospitalized for tests when she told her doctor about her joint pains, fatigue, and weight loss that had taken place over the previous six weeks. Her doctor found that she also had a fever of 105° F (40.5° C). In the hospital, blood tests showed that she was also dangerously anemic, her kidneys were functioning less than optimally, one eye and one lung were similarly affected, and there was measurable weakness in many of her joints. Alison has systemic lupus.

*Maria, age twenty-three.* Maria consulted her family doctor when she was told at a public clinic that a test for syphilis was positive—and was baffled by a subsequent report, after another blood test, that the first report was erroneous, that "these things sometimes happen." She did not know quite what to think, since there was in fact no reason for her to suspect that she could possibly have contracted a venereal disease. Her doctor found that she had a low fever, that her pulse was a bit fast (often associated with fever), and that her hands were unusually pale and cold; she mentioned that she had experienced some recent shortness of breath. Maria has systemic lupus.

*Georgette, age thirty-one.* An alarming pair of symptoms brought Georgette to the emergency room of a large metropolitan medical center: she was having trouble breathing, and there were strange and frightening pains in her chest. A number of diagnostic procedures were immediately performed. Georgette's chest X ray showed enlargement of the heart, a highly unusual condition in so young a woman. Further tests revealed inflammation of the pericardium, the membrane around the heart, with a collection of fluid. The fluid was removed surgically, and recovery was smooth. But it may occur again, and other problems have arisen since. Georgette has systemic lupus.

We could go on for many pages. Rashes, fever, joint pains, weight loss, fatigue, heart problems, anemia, kidney and sensory malfunction, and false-positive tests for syphilis are just a few of the many signs and symptoms with which lupus might begin or to which it might progress. Among others might be sun sensitivity, pleurisy and pneumonia, hair loss, mental or emotional problems, nausea and vomiting, jaundice, and—well, almost any adverse phenomenon imaginable. Depending upon the initial complaint, systemic lupus has been (and is) not infrequently diagnosed at first as another autoimmune disorder (especially scleroderma or rheumatoid arthritis), cancer, rheumatic fever, allergy, kidney infection, phlebitis —in fact, just about everything but the common cold.

Decades ago, syphilis—because its late-stage manifestations can be so varied and affect so many different parts of the body—was known as "the great imitator." Now the bacterium responsible for that venereal disease can be easily pinpointed and, with early testing and diagnosis, the infection can be banished, so that later, more advanced stages are rarely seen; the first stage of syphilis, in which there are typically clear and unmistakable symptoms, is now usually the stage of treatment.*

In children, some forms of leukemia are also known as "great imitators." Frequently, those cases that begin with mild symptoms can emulate a number of common childhood infections and can also assume the guise of common, nonserious injury to which youngsters are generally prone.

But *lupus* is now *the* "great imitator."

Among the first-recognized symptoms in three out of four cases of systemic lupus is mild but persistent aching in the joints—most commonly, finger joints, knuckles, wrists, or knees. Often, as in rheumatoid arthritis, the ache and stiffness are worst in the morning and may dissipate entirely later in the day. At least nine out of ten lupus patients will experience arthralgia (joint pain) and/or arthritis (actual joint inflammation) sooner or later, and about a quarter will suffer from muscle aches as well.

Some 20 to 25 percent first visit a physician because of puzzling symptoms involving the skin or mucous membranes. Sometimes a rash is on the face and assumes the classic "butterfly" form—but it may be almost anywhere, and

* The false-positive reaction to the test for syphilis, which we mentioned earlier—it can occur in some other conditions, notably acute hepatitis, as well as in lupus—is associated with the most widespread test in use, the RPR (for rapid plasma reagin). A very sensitive test which is highly unlikely to miss a case of syphilis, it is usually the initial test used by both private physicians and broad screening programs. If there is reason to suspect a false-positive reaction, a second, different type of test—called the FTA-ABS (for fluorescent treponemal antibody absorption)—may be used. (False-positive reactions to the FTA-ABS test, while not unknown, are extremely rare.)

legs and arms are common sites. About 85 percent of lupus patients will have skin or mucous membrane involvement eventually.

Typically (in about 80 percent) an unexplained, low but persistent fever is among the patient's initial symptoms (90 percent will run fevers at one time or another). Often the patient will report fatigue (about 75 percent) or weight loss along with loss of appetite (about two thirds), and there may also be any one or more of a variety of other complaints, including persistent swollen lymph nodes and unusual sensitivity to the sun (contrary to some published reports, a sizable number—about one third—of lupus patients, but *not* all, display this sensitivity).

Whatever the symptoms at the start of the illness, or at the time of diagnosis, compilations of past experience suggest that additional signs and symptoms are apt to occur eventually. Among these are hair loss (there is a probability of about 25 percent), cardiac problems of one sort or another (30 to 45 percent), pleuritis or pleurisy (45 to 50 percent), major kidney-function abnormalities (perhaps half), and others of which there is somewhat lower probability.

All or none of the above, it should be added, may occur in any one patient; the foregoing figures are statistics, not individual prognoses. But they have occurred and doubtless will continue to occur. And they are, one and all, due to the inflammatory process that marks the syndrome we call lupus: inflammation that may strike anywhere in the body, at any time; inflammation that is the hallmark of the illness; inflammation that is the evidence of the continuing battle taking place below the threshold of visibility, the attack of the body's defense mechanisms upon its own cells and structures.

No one yet knows what triggers or nurtures the cellular destruction (the second part of this book is devoted to speculation on this mystery), *except* for this fact: in approximately 10 to 12 percent of all diagnosed lupus cases, the appearance of the disease has followed the administration of one of a number of drugs. And, significantly, cessation of the drug has halted the lupus—cured it, if you will—at least after a time (treatment may be necessary). Spontaneous lupus, not associated with a drug, is generally chronic (as with rheumatoid arthritis, there are often "active" and "inactive" periods—and inactive periods may last for many years, or even indefinitely). Thus, in a small proportion of cases, the illness—though substantially the same at the time of its appearance as the chronic, non-drug-related cases—is clearly provoked by a specific agent. This similarity between the two types of lupus extends to laboratory findings, which will be discussed in the next chapter.

A number of different types of medication have been implicated in setting off the lupus process, and they have little or nothing in common that might provide hints to those seeking the cause of the "naturally" occurring disease. The best documented are procainamide (Procan, Pronestyl), a drug given to correct certain cardiac arrhythmias (irregularities of the heartbeat), which induces lupuslike disease in 25 to 30 percent of the patients who take it; hydralazine (Apresoline), a drug used to treat hypertension (high blood pressure); sulfonamides ("sulfa drugs"), used to treat certain infections; nitrofurantoin, used in some urinary-tract infections; isoniazid, an antituberculosis drug; and tetracycline used when it was outdated or had been improperly stored under high heat and humidity. Others that have uncommonly triggered symptoms of lupus or have been suspected of doing so include penicillamine (a drug used in rheumatoid arthritis), some tranquilizers, and various anticonvulsants. In many instances, there is *only* a suspicion, since a mere chronological relationship does not prove cause: the fact that X precedes Y doesn't mean that X necessarily causes Y, and a patient might have developed similar symptoms without the drug.

As far as symptoms are concerned, these drug-induced cases do differ somewhat from idiopathic lupus.† There is the

---

† "Idiopathic" is a widely used medical term coined from two Greek words that translate literally as "private, or personal, illness." Whatever the circumstances of the original coinage, it has come to denote any condition, whether suffered by one individual or by millions, for which no definite

same incidence of joint symptoms, the same likelihood of chest inflammation and congestion. As we noted, many abnormal laboratory findings are identical. And the majority of reported cases have been women—although the majority is a slim one compared with the numbers of women who account for 89 percent of lupus patients overall. In drug-caused lupus, however, there is little or no likelihood of swollen lymph nodes, of any kidney or gastrointestinal problems, or of any emotional or mental effects (which may occur in one in four cases of the "regular" kind of lupus), and the patient is only half as likely to have fever, a rash, anemia (a finding in perhaps half of all lupus patients), or heart involvement. These cases—of lupus, "drug-induced lupus," or, if you will, "pseudolupus"—almost invariably respond to conservative treatment consisting of withdrawal of the suspected drug and tiding the patient over with supportive medications and other therapies until symptoms have abated.

But, in the vast majority of cases, in a possible one million Americans, there is no such easy answer. In the next chapter, we take a closer look at what lupus is: what characterizes the syndrome at the cellular level and how it can be differentiated and distinguished from other ills with some similar symptoms.

---

cause can be pinpointed. The vast majority of lupus cases are of course in this category, as are most instances of epilepsy, high blood pressure, and many other ailments.

# 3. Singling It Out: Diagnostic Determinants

With such nebulous initial complaints as rashes, fevers, malaise, lack of appetite, and divers aches and pains, it might seem virtually impossible to arrive at a diagnosis of systemic lupus. But diagnosis, as in any condition requiring therapy, is necessary so that appropriate treatment can be instituted—and, as important, so that *in*appropriate, or even potentially harmful, measures are not taken.

Initial symptoms might seem, for example, to suggest a bacterial infection. But if the condition does *not* stem from bacterial infection, it will not be improved by the administration of antibiotics; if the patient has lupus and happens to have multiple allergies—as many lupus patients, in fact, do—and is specifically allergic to the antibiotic used, she may well become much sicker. (We've used "she" here, and will continue to do so, both to avoid repeated use of the cumbersome "he or she" and because the vast majority of people with lupus are women.)

Until the early 1970s, however, there were no established guidelines; lupus was diagnosed, or not diagnosed, on the basis of the individual physician's experience with its various manifestations. That experience, of course, might vary from quite broad to little or none. It is highly likely that a great many cases were not diagnosed at all (and many still are not).

In 1971, the Diagnostic and Therapeutic Criteria Committee of the American Rheumatism Association (ARA), the organization of physicians specializing in the rheumatic and arthritic disorders, set about the task of establishing diagnostic criteria. Calling upon leading rheumatologists throughout the United States and Canada, the committee drew up a list of characteristics—symptoms and complaints, clinical observations, and laboratory findings—that had, in the experience of the reporting doctors, occurred with significant frequency in lupus patients, based upon detailed case histories. All these characteristics were then laboriously compared with findings in an equal number of rheumatic-disorder patients who did not have lupus and still another group in which there was no suspicion of any rheumatoid disorder.

There were nearly sixty items in all, but obviously some were more significant than others. Peripheral neuritis (inflammation of nerves outside the central nervous system), for example, was reported in 11.4 percent of lupus patients, but it was also found in 8.2 percent of rheumatoid arthritis patients—not a substantial difference, and so clearly a rather poor criterion upon which to base a suspicion of lupus. Pleuritis, on the other hand, was found to occur in 60 percent of lupus patients but in fewer than 10 percent of the other groups—a marked difference, making it highly significant in diagnosing lupus.

The committee eventually winnowed the list to fourteen criteria but, as we observed in the first edition of this book, a number of questions were raised. The criteria were criticized on two scores. One was the inclusion of signs and symptoms that seemed to some not sufficiently specific: while firm confirmation of four criteria were required for diagnosis of lupus, it was pointed out that occasionally certain combinations of four of the criteria might appear in rheumatoid arthritis or some other condition. At the same time, a chronic lupus sufferer might at any given moment evidence only one or two. Secondly, certain other findings well known to be associated with lupus were *not* included among the criteria because the information was not available for a large proportion of the cases considered by the committee and their inclusion would not therefore have been scientifically valid.

The 1971 criteria did nevertheless constitute a good and helpful start and served as a useful basis for further study and refinement of the guidelines. As more experience was gained, and more sophisticated laboratory tests developed, it became evident that some criteria were far more significant than others—in medical terms, offering demonstrably greater *specificity*.

A word of explanation, before we go on to discuss today's diagnosis of lupus, on diagnostic testing in general. It relies essentially on two factors, *sensitivity* and *specificity*.

Let us say that a particular factor, which we'll call X, is found in 90 percent of all those who have a particular disease. An accurate test for factor X would be positive in nine out of every ten people with the disease (and would give a false-negative result in the tenth person with the disease). But if that same factor is also found in, say, 40 percent of people who do *not* have the disease, a test for factor X would also be positive in four out of ten healthy people—*falsely* positive, so far as diagnosing the disease is concerned. A test for factor X would be described as highly *sensitive*, since it would "miss" only 10 percent of those with the disease—but its *specificity* would be quite low, since it would be of little help in pinpointing a definite diagnosis.

Or, let us say that factor Y is found in 50 percent of people with a certain disease but in only 1 percent of those who do not have the disease. An accurate test for factor Y would have low *sensitivity*, since it would "miss" fully half of those with the disease—i.e., those without factor Y; such a test would be useless in broad screening of a population in a search for cases of the disease. But it would be far more *specific* than the test for factor X, since the finding of factor Y would suggest a 99-to-1 probability that the disease was present.

Ideally, a diagnostic test would be 100 percent sensitive and 100 percent specific: no one with the disease would be "missed" (there would be no false-negative results), and no one without the disease would be believed afflicted with it (there would be no false-positives). Unfortunately, no such test exists for lupus, because thus far, no X or Y factor has been identified that *is* found in all those who have lupus and is *not* found in anyone else (although, as we'll see, there are promising candidates). Thus, a combination of findings are still necessary to establish the diagnosis.

Those findings, under the revised criteria issued by the ARA in 1982, now number eleven. Again, the presence of four—not necessarily simultaneously—is considered the requisite for establishing the diagnosis without question. While the new criteria are said to offer combined sensitivity and specificity of 96 percent, they too will have to stand or fall on the basis of further clinical experience and may be still further revised in the future. And, as was true with the earlier guidelines, there are factors *not* included in (or now dropped from) the guidelines which will nonetheless be taken into account by experienced physicians in dealing with individual patients. We shall comment on the major ones. But first, the eleven new criteria (here paraphrased in some instances and including some explanatory language):

1. The classic "butterfly rash" over the nose and cheeks, possibly only on one side of the face.

2. Reddish raised patches, anywhere on the body, characteristic of what was traditionally known as "discoid" lupus and is now considered a possible form or manifestation of the systemic condition. (The latter may or may not develop.) These lesions are roughly disc-shaped, thick, and scaly; they may leave scars after healing. They occur in about 15 percent of lupus patients.

3. Photosensitivity—a skin rash resulting from an unusual reaction to sunlight.

4. Ulcerative sores in the mouth or throat; they are usually painless.

5. Arthritis—joint inflammation—involving two or more peripheral joints (such joints include all those of the hands, arms, feet, and legs, as well as those of the hips, shoulders, and lower jaw). The symptoms include pain on motion, tenderness, and swelling.

6. Evidence of either pleuritis (inflammation of the pleura, the membrane lining the chest cavity) or pericarditis (inflammation of the pericardium, the outer membrane surrounding the heart).

7. Evidence of renal (kidney) disorder. This may consist of either of two findings. One is a persistent high level of proteinuria (the presence of certain proteins in the urine, as determined by laboratory tests); it may be symptomatic of a number of conditions, but it is always considered in conjunction with other findings. The second is the finding in the urine of cellular casts, fragments of elements normally found in the blood—suggesting minute foci of bleeding within the kidney.

8. Signs of neurologic disorder, which may be either seizures or psychosis, occurring without any other explanation such as ingestion of a toxic drug, injury, or metabolic derangement.

9. Hematologic abnormalities—specified deficits in the various types of blood cells. This may consist of hemolytic anemia (anemia caused by too rapid destruction of red blood cells), thrombocytopenia (a deficit in thrombocytes or platelets, the "clotting cells"), or leukopenia (a deficit in white cells).

10. Findings pointing to immunologic disorders, which may be any of four: a false-positive reaction to the standard test for syphilis, persisting for at least six months and confirmed as false by the more specific FTA-ABS test (see note, page 11); a positive LE-cell test; the presence of anti-DNA; or the presence of anti-Sm. (We'll explain the last three at the end of the list.)

11. An abnormal level of antinuclear antibodies, in the absence of drugs known to induce lupuslike disease (see Chapter 2).

The last was an important factor missing from the 1971 ARA criteria. As most readers doubtless know, antibodies are, generally speaking, defense forces developed by the body in response to antigens—factors perceived as threatening or foreign. They are highly specific. A measles vaccination—or, for that matter, the illness itself—will result in the development of antibodies only against that particular virus. Other immunizations utilizing antigenic materials, such as those for polio, rubella, and flu, work exactly the same way.

These antigen-antibody reactions are, of course, extremely helpful, since they protect the body against subsequent attack by disease-causing organisms.

Since the late 1950s, there has been noted in lupus patients extremely high levels of a different class of antibodies called antinuclear antibodies (ANA)—antibodies that act not against specific disease-causing agents but indiscriminately against the nuclear material of cells. These antibodies do not penetrate living cells; rather, they apparently react to proteins, liberated from cells, that act as antigens. It is quite possible that the inflammatory lesions of the kidneys, lymph nodes, spleen, and other sites seen in lupus are the result of the deposition at these sites of circulating antigen-antibody complexes—which might be visualized as pockets of combat activity between these two elements.

Tests for ANA have, at any rate, proved positive in over 90 percent of lupus patients (percentages have varied with the studies reported), but in fewer than 5 percent of other individuals. (An exception: rheumatoid arthritis patients, as many as two thirds of whom may have ANA. The levels are nearly always lower, however, than in patients with active lupus.) This finding was not included in the 1971 criteria, because unfortunately such data were not uniformly available in the cases considered by the committee, and the inclusion would not have been statistically valid.

Now, to the promised explanation of the three mysterious terms in criterion number 10. First, the LE cell.

The year 1948 marked a milestone in rheumatology. In that year, Dr. Malcolm M. Hargraves and his colleagues at the Mayo Clinic discovered and described a new and unique phenomenon. In material isolated from the bone marrow of a lupus patient, stained in a specific manner and placed on a microscope slide, they saw a particular type of white cell called a polymorphonuclear leukocyte, its nuclear substance pushed to one side by another such cell nucleus within it— essentially, a cell devouring the nuclear material of another of its kind. This evidence of aberrant phagocytosis (a process by which white cells normally dispose of bacteria, body discards, and other cellular debris), which can now be found by blood sampling, is the LE cell—also sometimes referred to as the LE factor or the LE phenomenon.

LE cells are not found in all lupus patients; they appear, however, in perhaps 80 percent at one time or another, according to recent ARA figures, especially when the disease process is active (as previously noted, there is a flare-and-remission pattern in lupus). Further, they are only very rarely found in anyone who does not have lupus: the 1971 ARA committee study found LE cells reported in fewer than 4 percent of the rheumatoid arthritis cases and in a mere 0.5 percent of the third, nonrheumatoid patient group. (LE cells are also sometimes found in certain other conditions, notably some systemic fungal infections. And of course it is perfectly possible that these patients may have had lupus, previously unsuspected because of atypically mild symptoms.) Thus the LE-cell phenomenon, while not an absolute guarantee—either by its presence or its absence—of correct diagnosis, is a highly specific finding.

Next, anti-DNA. The terms DNA (deoxyribonucleic acid) and RNA (ribonucleic acid) are doubtless familiar to the reader. These are the active materials in cells, particularly in cell replication (they are released as well, of course, in cell disintegration), and it is to these substances, among others, that the ANAs react. Each is found with two different molecular structures, which are known as "double-stranded" and "single-stranded."

Double-stranded DNA is sometimes called "native" DNA, since it is a basic constituent of human cells; antibodies to it—sometimes written "anti-dsDNA"—are found frequently in active stages of lupus and in 70 to 80 percent of all lupus patients at some time, but only occasionally in other conditions. (Antibodies to single-stranded DNA can be found in a probable 90 percent of lupus patients, but are also found in patients with rheumatoid arthritis and other connective-tissue disorders.) In 1976, Dr. M. Edward Medof and his colleagues at the University of Chicago Pritzker School of Medicine, reporting on their study of this phenomenon over a three-year period, suggested that more sophisticated testing methods may show that high titers (measurements of antibody levels in the blood) of antibodies to double-stranded DNA do not occur in *any* other conditions and that this finding is uniquely specific to lupus; others have since echoed that thought. In fact, one study reported in 1983, comparing two laboratory techniques used for this purpose, found one demonstrated 100 percent specificity for lupus; i.e., anti-dsDNA was not found in any nonlupus patients.

Double-stranded RNA, unlike double-stranded DNA, is normally found only in trace amounts in the tissues of mammals but occurs in significant quantities in certain viruses (a fact upon which we'll comment further in a later chapter). Antibodies to double-stranded RNA have, again, been found in about half the patients with lupus but very uncommonly in other conditions.

Finally, anti-Sm, a complete newcomer to the diagnostic scene. Sm is a nuclear protein, and while tests for anti-Sm antibody are not particularly sensitive—it is found in fewer than 50 percent of lupus patients overall (although some studies have reported as high as 58 percent)—it is believed to be possibly totally specific for lupus. As with anti-dsDNA, this may be confirmed in the future by the use of more sophisticated testing methods. (Sm, by the way, is not a medical abbreviation. It is an arbitrary designation taken from the name of the patient in whom it was first identified.)

The ARA guidelines call for four of the criteria to be met in order to declare the diagnosis of lupus definite. But they need not occur simultaneously, and over a given period of time, only two or three might be evident. Presumably, a fourth might emerge eventually—but until it does, is the practicing physician at a complete loss? Not really. As we commented earlier, there are other factors the knowledgeable rheumatologist will consider.

Two of these were included in the ARA's earlier preliminary criteria. One is rapidly occurring, unexplained alopecia —loss of hair from the scalp. Hair loss can stem from many, many causes, ranging from mechanical stress to toxins, allergies, emotional duress, and infections such as ringworm of the scalp—so, like fever and loss of appetite (which were never among the criteria), it offers very low sensitivity *and* specificity vis-à-vis lupus.

The second is a condition known as *Raynaud's phenomenon*—paling and numbing of the fingers (less commonly, the toes) due to interference with circulation to the small arteries of the hands (or feet); it is essentially identical to frostbite, although the same climatic conditions need not obtain. It occurs in about 30 percent of lupus patients—and it is also found in patients suffering from several other connective-tissue disorders, so, like hair loss, it can't serve to single out lupus. In fact, it can even exist all by itself, unrelated to any systemic condition—in which case it is called Raynaud's *syndrome* or Raynaud's *disease.*

Raynaud's phenomenon is a frequent feature of scleroderma, another autoimmune disorder which often may be confused with lupus and which is characterized by the skin's becoming hard and leatherlike in appearance. Almost all scleroderma patients have ANA—but anti-dsDNA antibodies, found in the vast majority of lupus patients, are extremely rare in scleroderma.

There are also some additional laboratory findings that a physician may find helpful:

*Free DNA.* A corollary to the ANAs clue is a finding of free (circulating) DNA. As we've said, the antibodies do not penetrate living cells, but interact only with liberated nuclear material. High free-DNA levels, while not specifically diagnostic (for lupus or any other condition), certainly point to abnormal cell-demolition activity.

*Immunoglobulins.* These are the substances found in blood serum that actually contain antibodies. While the most widely mentioned, in print and elsewhere, is *gamma* globulin (sometimes for purposes of deliberate simplification), there are actually a number of such substances. There appear, by and large, to be abnormally high overall immunoglobulin levels in lupus patients, particularly during inflammatory exacerbations (in some instances *only* at those times), and the relationship with proteinuria, one of the aforementioned criteria, is statistically significant.

In the case of gamma globulin, however, some researchers have found elevated levels in a majority of lupus patients even without marked disease activity. And dermatological studies have found deposits of three particular immunoglobulins, designated IgA, IgG, and IgM, at the juncture of the upper level (epidermis) and second level (dermis) of the skin in 92 percent of rash-afflicted skin analyzed—*and* in 60 percent of tests performed on uninvolved skin. The rate for a control group was 5 percent. (In discoid lupus that has not progressed to the systemic type, this deposition does *not* occur in uninvolved skin.)

*Rheumatoid factor.* There is, as we've already seen, some symptomatic overlap between lupus and other connective-tissue disorders, notably rheumatoid arthritis. A procedure called a latex fixation test will reveal a blood element (it's classified as a kind of antibody and is found in gamma globulin) called the rheumatoid factor in approximately 75 to 80 percent of rheumatoid arthritis patients (though not usually during the first year of illness). The test is also positive in about 15 percent of lupus patients, as well as in a quarter to a third of scleroderma patients and up to 40 percent of those with polymyositis.* Its value is thus limited, but many physicians feel it is helpful in conjunction with other findings.

*Sedimentation rate.* Another blood test may also sometimes be employed; this is determination of the erythrocyte sedimentation rate, often abbreviated to ESR or simply "sed rate." It measures the sinking velocity of red cells within a quantity of drawn blood—and here, too, there is considerable overlap with the rheumatoid arthritis picture. The ESR is elevated in about 90 percent of patients with that disorder and also in a reported 85 to 95 percent of lupus patients. (It

---

* Polymyositis ("inflammation of many muscles") is an autoimmune disorder in which muscle weakness is the most prominent symptom and in which a lupuslike rash may sometimes occur. In polymyositis, the most helpful elements in differential diagnosis are blood analyses for certain enzymes freed in the course of muscle breakdown.

should be noted, though, that reported results have not been consistent: some researchers have found the ESR high only when the disease was especially active, while others have found it perfectly normal even during such periods. Further, this value may be affected by any blood-cell deficits that may be present. And elevated rates can occur, too, in many infections, not excluding the common cold.)

*Serum complement.* A series of at least nine proteins (that number have thus far been identified), normally present in the blood, constitute what Nobel Prize-winning bacteriologist and immunologist Paul Ehrlich christened the complement system. Many, though not all, immunological reactions are dependent upon these proteins for their successful completion: attracted by antigen-antibody complexes, the "pockets of combat activity" we mentioned earlier, these proteins move in and, acting in a cascadelike manner, provide "backup" aid for the antibodies by destroying the cell membranes of the "enemy" organisms. Thus, in lupus, complement is drawn to the areas of self-destructive activity—and, because the total amount of complement in the body at any given moment is finite, there will be lower-than-normal levels circulating in the blood at such times, and a low serum-complement level is indicative of active disease. For that reason, determination of the level is helpful not only in diagnosis but in treatment as well, and the level is often monitored during therapy; a falling value may suggest increasing disease activity even before symptoms become evident, while rising levels of serum complement are typically correlated with improvement and can thus confirm the effectiveness of medication.

*Other antibodies.* Sm, which we mentioned earlier, is one of a number of substances collectively known as nuclear proteins or extractable nuclear antigens (ENAs); others include Ro, La (like Sm, arbitrary designations reflecting patients' names), and nRNP (for nuclear ribonucleoprotein). The last has proved somewhat useful. About 40 to 45 percent of lupus patients have anti-nRNP antibodies (for anti-Ro and anti-La, the figures are only about 30 and 15 percent, respectively), often together with anti-Sm.

There is an entity, first described in the 1970s, which is as yet ill-defined and seems to include features of lupus as well as several other connective-tissue disorders (notably sclero-derma and polymyositis); it is known, for want of a better term, as "mixed connective-tissue disease" (MCTD). MCTD patients invariably have anti-nRNP antibodies; in fact, that is the only consistent feature of the syndrome. Most do not have anti-Sm antibodies. Basically, anti-nRNP antibodies are associated more with certain signs and symptoms (including arthritis in several joints, Raynaud's phenomenon, positive ANA, and a low incidence of serious kidney problems, among others) than with diagnosis per se. But in cases that are diagnostically confusing, checking for antibodies to other ENAs besides Sm can help to differentiate one connective-tissue disorder from another.

Comparisons of the levels of various antibodies may also eventually prove helpful in prognosis—hence, treatment as well; thus far, for example, the presence of anti-nRNP anti-bodies appears to be associated with milder disease.

Anti-nRNP, incidentally, is also found in drug-induced lu-pus, but in only about 20 percent of the cases, while an-tinuclear antibodies are found in the same proportion as in idiopathic lupus. Anti-Sm and anti-dsDNA antibodies are not found in drug-induced lupus at all; since they are believed probably specific to lupus itself, this would seem to indicate a definite difference between the two conditions.

We shall return to some of these diagnostic factors in Part Two, as we discuss further research findings.

# PART TWO:
# THE CLUES

A number of mysterious ailments of the past, typically multisymptomatic ills, have provoked speculation as to cause and cure. It should be noted that determination of the first has almost invariably preceded the second. Exceptions have been purely fortuitous, such as the ancient Chinese predilection for tea drinking on the premise that the beverage was of divine inspiration and promoted well-being by encouraging a continuing internal harmony. In fact, boiling the water used to make the tea probably prevented a great many serious afflictions acquired by imbibing water directly from streams of doubtful purity. But, by and large, discovery of the identity of a disease-causing agent or circumstance has ultimately led to successful efforts to prevent or cure the affliction.

Earlier, we mentioned syphilis; it is an excellent example. At its various stages, symptoms of syphilis may include skin lesions of various types, heart and circulatory malfunctions, ulcerations of the respiratory tract, arthritis, severe muscle pains, extensive hair loss, deterioration of the central nervous system, blindness, skeletal deformities, and psychosis.

Although syphilis had probably been observed in one form or another throughout recorded history (some of its manifestations were probably included in the biblical "leprosy"), it was first recognized as a single disease entity in the late fifteenth century. Naturally, there was immediate pronouncement as to the cause—which was, the Holy Roman Emperor Maximilian declared in 1495, clearly divine reprisal for blasphemy, hence its designation, in that era of holierthan-the-next-nation rivalries, as "the French disease," "the Spanish disease," "the Portuguese disease," "the German disease," "the disease of the Turks," etc. (Incidentally, the French—when they were not calling it "the Italian disease" —came to refer to syphilis as "the pox" and specifically the "great" pox, as compared with the other dreaded epidemic ill prevalent at that time. Which is how smallpox got its name.) Subsequent theories included astrologically plotted planetary transits (a conjunction of Mars and Saturn was particularly suspect) and atmospheric phenomena, including both extreme humidity and severe drought.

It was not until the first decade of the twentieth century that the spirochete responsible for syphilis was discovered, although the fact that the disease was clearly contagious, and the mode of transmission, had been established in the interim. Specifics against syphilis, notably an arsenic compound called Salvarsan, were soon introduced. Such drugs, despite their many and serious side effects, remained in use until the 1940s, when the effectiveness of penicillin was unarguably demonstrated.*

While lupus has been generally recognized as a disease entity, some still feel that it may represent a spectrum of diseases. No mode of either acquisition or transmission is known. No pathogen or other villain has been identified.

But there are clues—and tentative theories. Since this is the twentieth century and not the fifteenth, the speculations involve neither divine retribution, planetary vibrations, nor climatic events (although the possibility of other environmental factors can't be, and hasn't been, excluded). In the following five chapters, we single out the most provocative observations and what may be the most promising lines of current medical research. Which may, we should add, seem primitive, naïve, or plainly misguided when—a decade, a century, or more from now—the answer becomes evident.

---

* Readers interested in exploring further the intriguing medical and social history of venereal disease will find Theodor Rosebury's *Microbes and Morals* (Ballantine, 1973) both entertaining and informative.

# 4. Sex Discrimination

The demographics of lupus cannot be ignored. There is a rheumatoid condition, gout, that affects more men than women. And there are many congenital conditions—color blindness and hemophilia are certainly the best known, but there are quite a few others—that, because of a mechanism called X-linked recessive inheritance, afflict a marked preponderance of males. There are certain other connective-tissue disorders affecting more women than men, including rheumatoid arthritis, in which the ratio is an estimated three to one. But in no other known disease or disorder are such an overwhelming majority of the victims female. (We have ignored obvious exceptions specifically involving the reproductive system of one sex or the other.)

Estimates differ as to the extent of the disproportion. Several studies of large populations in recent years, however, have suggested a disparity greater than earlier impressions; it now appears that at *least* eight out of nine, or 89 percent, of lupus sufferers are women.

Further, there is a distinct preference for what are generally referred to as the "childbearing" years, the years between menarche and menopause. Although lupus has been diagnosed in both small children and senior citizens, the concentration of cases is from the teens to the forties, with a mean onset age of about twenty-nine or thirty. During these years, the ratio of women to men among lupus patients is at least ten to one and, according to some estimates, may be as high as fifteen to one. After the age of about fifty-five, the gender imbalance drops to about two to one. And the mean age of diagnosis in men is much higher than in women—fifty-one years.

Essentially, then, there is a dual phenomenon: a preference for the female of the species and a concentration on her reproductive period.

The immediately evident question: Has lupus any association with estrogens, the hormones produced chiefly by females and produced in greatest quantity during this span of years? The quantity produced declines after menopause—and it is then, as we've noted, that lupus's sex discrimination lessens as well.

It has long been postulated that the female hormones play a protective role in certain other conditions. These include both ailments that afflict a vastly greater number of men—coronary heart disease, for example—and others, including breast cancer, that strike postmenopausal women much more frequently than younger ones. Precisely the reverse pattern prevails in lupus.

Estrogen deficiencies certainly do not *cause* either heart attacks or malignancies. But these hormones *may*, as we've said, play some *protective* role. One might then ask if, in lupus, the reverse situation obtains: if perhaps androgens, the male hormones, play some part in protecting *males*. The vast majority of women, of course, are never struck by lupus. So that two corollary questions might be whether unusually *high* levels of estrogen are secreted by women who have lupus—and/or lower-than-normal androgen levels by male lupus patients.

It is interesting, in this regard, to note that lupus is found disproportionately often in men with the congenital disorder called Klinefelter's syndrome. In this condition, which occurs in at least one in every thousand male births and perhaps as many as one in five hundred, the male embryo has somehow picked up an extra X chromosome (the disorder is accidental, not hereditary). The normal male's sex-chromosome pattern is XY, the female's XX; the pattern in Klinefelter's is XXY (so long as a Y is present, the individual is still male). Often, the condition becomes evident only at puberty, since the major effect is on sexual development; it is treated by administration of male hormones.

But deficiencies are not always what they seem. Vitamin "deficiencies," for example, may stem not from lack of those elements in the diet but from inability to absorb or metabolize certain foods. Many cases of diabetes mellitus are due not to underproduction of insulin but to apparent inability to utilize the hormone normally.

Indeed, if hormones per se were responsible for lupus, one would expect to find distinct departures from normal levels in normal (XY) males with lupus. Extensive hormone profiles of lupus patients have not been undertaken, but some small groups have been investigated. One interesting study of eight such male patients was reported in 1982 by Drs. Robert Inman and Michael Lockshin of Cornell University Medical College and their colleagues. The eight patients' levels of both major androgens (male hormones) and major estrogens (female hormones) were carefully checked.

The results were something less than conclusive. Of the eight, only one had a testosterone (the major male hormone) level below the normal range. Findings for other androgens: dyhydroepiandrosterone, none below normal; androstenedione, four of the eight slightly below normal; dihydrotestosterone, two markedly below normal, three very slightly below normal, one in the normal range, and two markedly *above* that range (those two patients' other levels were all normal). ("Slightly," as we've used it here, is a very minute quantity. Hormone levels were measured in nanograms—billionths of a gram—per deciliter, and "very slightly" means one or two ng.)

As to the two major estrogens: While four of the eight patients did have both estrone and estradiol levels above the normal range, the estrone levels for three other patients were *lower* than normal, and one of those had lower-than-normal estradiol levels as well. Further, one of the high-estrogen patients was one of those who had higher-than-normal dihydrotestosterone levels. And the androgen profile of the patient whose estrogens were both below the normal range showed only a slightly below normal departure in levels of one of those four hormones.

So much for strictly quantitative measurements. But, as with vitamins and insulin, might the way the body handles these hormones make a difference? Dr. Robert G. Lahita of Rockefeller University thinks so and has documented apparent abnormalities in metabolism of sex hormones in both male and female lupus patients. In one such study, published in 1982, Dr. Lahita and his colleagues injected both lupus patients (five men and five women) and a group of healthy volunteers (eleven men and eighteen women) with estradiol and testosterone.

Lupus patients of both sexes, he found, metabolized— chemically broke down—estradiol differently from the volunteers, as determined by measuring the proportions of the various breakdown components (metabolites) they excreted. The most marked difference was in the percentage of a metabolite called 16 alpha-hydroxyestrone—5 to 5.2 percent for the volunteer controls, but 16.9 percent for the male lupus patients and 20.6 percent for the females. This metabolite, he postulated, rather than the estradiol itself, may play a significant role in lupus.

With testosterone, which is eventually oxidized by the body to the estrogens estradiol and estrone, Dr. Lahita examined the extent of oxidization. Again, there was a difference. Although there was some overlap, the mean figure for lupus patients was 83 percent, that for the volunteers 63 percent.

In short, individuals with lupus may convert more testosterone to estrogen—and, in turn, may then convert more of that estrogen to a potentially troublemaking metabolite. If so —what part does that metabolite play in causing, encouraging, or exacerbating the disease? That is yet to be discovered. And *why* are these hormones handled differently by lupus patients? The answer to that may lie in the largely unmapped realm of heredity, which we'll be exploring in the next chapter.

On the other hand, an entirely different theory regarding

the sex imbalance has been put forth in some quarters: that lupus *would* strike equal numbers of men and women among those susceptible to it (presuming hereditary susceptibility), but that an inordinate number of males in that category simply do not survive long enough to contract the condition. Many of those incipient victims, it is postulated, either succumb during gestation—i.e., are miscarried or stillborn—or, for one reason or another, do not survive childhood.

One investigator pursued this question by seeking out the living siblings of a series of almost two hundred lupus patients, managing to contact 580. While he did not find a significant preponderance of females among the siblings in general, he did find such a preponderance among those siblings born immediately before, or immediately after, the lupus patients. And there had *not* been an extraordinary number of infant and childhood deaths among the patients' brothers. His conclusion: there had possibly been some factor in their mothers' lives (or environments) at that time that had a fatal effect upon male fetuses, while the same factor had had a different impact upon female fetuses—not causing any immediate difficulties but leading to the development of lupus later in life.

Some food for further thought along hormonal lines, in any case, might be found in some of the data regarding pregnancy and lupus. This subject has been investigated by a great many researchers, since it has touched the lives of so many lupus patients.

Children born to lupus patients display only a slightly higher incidence of one congenital heart problem (see Chapter 11). There *have* been, however, a much lower proportion of children-to-be actually carried to term. At least 10 percent of all diagnosed pregnancies, it is estimated, end in spontaneous abortion or, as it is popularly termed, miscarriage; the rate in lupus patients, according to various studies, has run as high as 30 percent, typically from 17 to 24 percent (and sometimes, lupus has been diagnosed only after repeated miscarriages). Further, about one in four babies born to lupus patients arrives prematurely, compared to an overall rate of about 8 percent.

As to the effect of pregnancy on the patient herself, conclusions of various reports have differed. Most, however, have concluded that chances for remission, worsening of the condition, or no change at all are not markedly affected by the pregnancy itself (although there appears a greater likelihood of flare-up during the first trimester and to some extent during the second). But there is a significant possibility of serious worsening of the lupus *following* pregnancy, when production of progesterone, increased relative to estrogen during pregnancy, slackens (and many physicians warn patients against becoming pregnant unless there has already been a lengthy remission). The probability for severe postpartum illness is especially great in a patient who has already suffered cardiac or kidney involvement. We'll be discussing pregnancy further, along with family planning, in Part Three.

# 5. Family Affairs

A great deal of speculation has centered on the possible role of heredity in lupus. Clearly, there is not a direct mode of inheritance as there is in a number of traits ranging from blood type, eye color, and dwarfism to disorders such as cystic fibrosis, color blindness, and sickle-cell anemia. But there are many ailments in which a predisposition or susceptibility is known or strongly suspected to be inherited, although the mechanism is not wholly understood; among them are diabetes mellitus, migraine, psoriasis, epilepsy, and most allergies.

One avenue of investigation has been that of examining and testing close relatives of lupus patients in search of either other cases of lupus or characteristics associated with lupus and/or other rheumatic disorders. The search has proved fruitful: there have been many reports detailing just such findings, far too many to attribute them to mere coincidence.

Typically, these studies have turned up not especially large numbers of lupus sufferers but constellations of unusual findings. One such study, for example, involved a lupus patient with an unusually large group of relatives available for study. The patient's mother, although she did not have lupus, did evidence hyperimmunoglobulinemia (as we noted in Chapter 3, a characteristic finding in lupus). Additionally, one of the patient's four sisters had diagnosed systemic lupus, and two other sisters and a brother hyperimmunoglobulinemia. There were no abnormal findings in the patient's two young daughters, but among nieces and nephews (at the time of the report, most were under the age of twelve years) were one girl with lupus, one girl with rheumatoid factor, a boy with both rheumatoid factor and hyperimmunoglobulinemia, and five more boys and a girl with hyperimmunoglobulinemia. All of these findings are far in excess of random determinations in the general population.

Similarly, a Scandinavian researcher delved into the families of 72 lupus patients, comparing close blood relatives with relations by marriage, who served as controls. In a 1972 report, the investigator recorded that the close blood relatives exhibited important lupus-associated features. These included 22 percent of the patients' daughters and 4.5 percent of their sons (but none of the offspring of the control group), as well as 24 percent of their sisters (the control-group rate was 9 percent). Again, the sex bias we discussed in the previous chapter is evident.

There have been quite a few reports of identical (monozygotic, originating from a single fertilized egg cell) twins with lupus—a significant point, because identical twins are identical not merely in appearance but in genetic inheritance.

An interesting sidelight, related to the speculation on the role of hormones discussed in Chapter 4, emerged in a case reported in 1975 in the *Journal of the American Rheumatism Association,* a case involving a lupus patient whose identical twin had *not* developed the condition. The women were forty-four at the time of the report. One had had lupus since the age of thirty-seven, and her tests for LE cells and antinuclear antibodies were positive; her sister's were negative. *Both,* however, displayed the classic false-positive reaction to the standard test for syphilis (the more accurate FTA-ABS test was negative for both), and both had unusually high immunoglobulin levels, in particular IgM. But the factor that struck the investigators was that the twin who did not have lupus had been successfully treated for ovarian cancer at the age of twenty-one; her treatment had involved oophorectomy and hysterectomy—removal of both ovaries and uterus (she had not been given hormone-replacement therapy).

When twins are found to exhibit a particular trait in common, they are said to be *concordant* for that trait; if one has the trait and the other does not, they are *discordant*. Overall, the reported concordance rate for lupus in monozygotic twins is approximately 70 percent—compared with a mere 3 percent in dizygotic ("fraternal") twins, who originate from two different fertilized egg cells and are no more closely related genetically than two siblings of different ages. Why only 70 percent? Why not 100 percent? There was one case, reported in the USSR about a decade ago, in which twins who had been orphaned and were separated at the age of six months and brought up by two different families—said to live in very different environments—both developed lupus at the age of fourteen, within a month of each other. Most identical twins are *not* separated as infants, however, and the fact that the concordance for lupus is not 100 percent suggests that while the *susceptibility* is inherited, lupus itself is not an inherited disorder: that there must be some other factor that triggers the actual disease in susceptible individuals.

Another aspect of the heredity hypothesis is the observation, which has been made by many, that the incidence of lupus appears to be increasing. This is a somewhat speculative area. As with other disorders presenting difficulties in definition and diagnosis, technological advance and the development of highly sophisticated diagnostic techniques have made possible far more accurate case-finding. The development of increasingly specific diagnostic criteria—such as the LE-cell phenomenon and anti-dsDNA and anti-Sm antibodies—has certainly been a key factor, and so have modern methods of serological analysis. It is thus very hard to determine whether a remarkable increase in reported cases reflects actual rising incidence, improvements in diagnosis, or simply broader reporting of cases due to heightened interest in the disorder. Certainly the last two elements are involved as far as lupus is concerned, and possibly all three.

If the statistics indeed reflect true rising incidence, many observers feel that it would tend to support the heredity theory. Certain other disorders in which the condition, or a predisposition, is without question inherited have in fact been increasing. The reason: improvements in therapy that have prolonged life and permitted greater opportunity for victims to pass on the genetic factors involved. A prominent example is diabetes mellitus. Prior to the advent of insulin therapy in the 1920s, the vast majority of insulin-dependent diabetics did not survive long enough to produce any significant number of offspring. Since that time, such individuals have grown to adulthood, many have become parents, and the incidence of diabetes mellitus has in fact risen dramatically. Successful medical management of conditions such as cystic fibrosis (which is directly heritable) suggests that statistics will shortly reflect rising incidence there as well. Similarly, there have been marked advances in the treatment of lupus over the past two and one half decades, with vast improvement in prognosis and life expectancy. The majority of lupus patients now live active, productive lives—and many have become parents.

The role of enzymes in familial disorders has received increasing attention in recent years. It has now been established that in several such congenital disorders—some evident immediately at birth, others not displaying signs or symptoms until months or even years thereafter—there are deficiencies in specific enzymes involved in the metabolism of certain lipids and proteins; these conditions include phenylketonuria, Tay-Sachs disease, Fabry's disease, and others.

No enzyme deficiency has been specially implicated as a causal factor in lupus. But there have been a number of studies of an enzyme called acetyltransferase, which is produced by the liver and is involved in a number of biochemical processes including metabolism of certain drugs. The activity of this enzyme can be revealed by determining the rate of breakdown of such drugs within the body; the longer the drug persists, the lower the level of activity. Individuals who metabolize these drugs quickly are known as *rapid acetylators;* those who take a relatively longer time are called *slow acetylators.* Whether one is a fast or slow acetylator is known to be genetically determined, and the U.S. population is more or less evenly divided between the two types.

Procainamide is one of the drugs handled by this enzyme —and, as we pointed out in Chapter 2, is the major drug known to cause drug-induced lupus. A number of studies have been done with procainamide, which can induce lupus —with a concomitant rise in antinuclear antibodies (ANA)— in both slow and rapid acetylators. But the time required is markedly different in the two groups. In one study, following a number of patients who were receiving procainamide for control of cardiac arrhythmias, all the slow acetylators had developed ANA within six months, while only a little over a third of the rapid acetylators had done so. Some of both groups developed lupuslike disease as well—but that took an average of four and one half years for the rapid acetylators, only one year for the slow acetylators.

Are there more slow acetylators among (non-drug-induced) lupus patients than in the general population? Various studies have come to different conclusions, but some of those were too small, perhaps, to be statistically representative. One recent review of all the published studies concluded that about two thirds of lupus patients are slow acetylators, significantly more than in the general population. What does this mean? No one is yet sure, but it *may* suggest—as Dr. Arthur Weinstein of the University of Connecticut School of Medicine recently hypothesized—that the agent or agents responsible for drug-induced lupus are specifically the unacetylated chemical fractions of the drugs. He points out that a variant of procainamide which has been pre-acetylated can be given to patients who had previously developed procainamide-induced lupus, and the syndrome does not recur.*

* Arthur Weinstein, "Lupus Syndromes Induced by Drugs," in *The Clinical Management of Systemic Lupus Erythematosus* (Grune & Stratton, 1983).
The variant is called acetylprocainamide. In 1983, it was assigned orphan drug status by the Food and Drug Administration. A drug so designated has potential value but is seeking a "parent"—someone to produce it so that it can be prescribed for patients; such a drug is typically one for which the market is relatively narrow and which no pharmaceutical firm has viewed as economically feasible to manufacture. Under the Orphan Drug Act, the government provides cost-cutting incentives, including tax credits, to en-

That, in turn, might hint that the agent or agents responsible for *idiopathic* lupus may have something in common chemically with the unacetylated fractions of the lupus-inducing drugs—hydrazines in the case of hydralazine, aromatic amines in the case of procainamide. We shall pursue this provocative thought further in Part Three.

The single most important new frontier in our exploration of the world of heredity, and of special relevance to lupus and other autoimmune disorders, is the discovery and investigation of the MHC, a.k.a. the HLA system.

Some years ago, in animal studies, it became evident that there existed a region, on a particular chromosome, controlling a number of immunological functions, including graft rejection and antibody responses. Because of its role in the acceptance or rejection of grafted tissue, it was dubbed the "major histocompatibility complex," MHC for short *(histos* is Greek for "tissue"). It was soon found that there was something of the same sort in people—a region, located on the sixth chromosome of every human cell, sometimes also called the HLA region (for "human leukocyte antigen," because it was first identified in white blood cells). As scientists have studied this tiny but highly complex genetic wonderland, they have pinpointed subregions—called HLA-A, HLA-B, and so on—and, within those subregions, certain biochemical "gene products" or "markers" that appear in some people but not in others and are, like blood groups ("types"), directly determined by heredity.

HLA "typing"—determination of histocompatibility—has become a major key to predicting the potential success of organ transplants, not to mention a high-tech resource in paternity suits. But there is another side to this analysis that can now tell scientists how much two people have or don't have in common and whether one might have fathered an-

---

courage production of these medications that are of little interest to most people but of very great interest to those few who might be helped by them. At this writing, a drug firm has expressed interest in further investigating acetylprocainamide.

other or is likely to be comfortable with another's kidney. It appears that the HLA region also governs, or at least relates to, susceptibility to certain disorders.

In the early 1970s, a team of California researchers began to look for a genetic key to ankylosing spondylitis, a crippling arthritis of the spine which strikes mostly men and had been observed to occur repeatedly in certain families. In 1973, they announced that they had found it: the marker designated HLA-B27, identified in 80 percent or more of spondylitis patients but in fewer than 10 percent of controls without the disease. It has since been suggested by some that those who have B27 but not the illness may eventually develop it.

In 1978, Dr. Peter Stastny of the University of Texas Health Science Center in Dallas announced what the Arthritis Foundation has termed "conclusive proof" that susceptibility to rheumatoid arthritis is inherited; the link, HLA-DRw4, was found in 70 percent of rheumatoid arthritis patients versus 28 percent of a control group—a difference that, while less dramatic than the B27 figures, is nonetheless statistically significant. These findings have since been confirmed by other researchers. In 1980, Dr. Stastny reported another study, of families in which at least two members had rheumatoid arthritis. In 75 percent, the disease was found in association with DRw4; in the others, it was linked with one of two closely associated markers, DRw3 or DRw5. And in early 1984, Dr. Barbara S. Nepom of Children's Orthopedic Hospital in Seattle reported finding what she described as a unique variant of DRw4 in children with an especially severe form of juvenile rheumatoid arthritis.

Such studies are not mere exercises in data accumulation. As Dr. Stastny had pointed out in connection with the 1980 study, the information could in the future be used in further studies, with prevention in mind: "For the first time, we now will be able to identify family members of rheumatoid arthritis patients who have the gene which predisposes to the disease but do not actually have the disease." Then, perhaps, if an infectious agent is found to cause the disease, those predisposed people might be protected by a vaccine against that agent.

Results of similar studies in lupus, thus far, have been less definitive; they have certainly not narrowed the focus to a single HLA-complex marker. There does, however, appear to be an association in lupus with DRw2 or DRw3 or both, as well as a somewhat more tenuous connection with A1 and B8. The reported figures have varied, but in one combination of three studies conducted at major centers in the United States, DRw2 was found in 53.7 percent of lupus patients versus 26.1 percent of controls; the proportions for DRw3 were 45.1 percent and 20.4 percent. Some studies have considered both together, on an either-or-both basis. One such investigation found either DRw2 or DRw3 or both in 73.6 percent of patients versus 42.6 percent of controls; in another, the figures were 85.7 percent versus 48.6 percent.

A few researchers, assuming that a combination of factors is operative (which seems likely in this multifaceted disorder), have sought a *haplotype*—a multilocus MHC expression. The one which it appears may be significant is A1-B8-DRw3, found by one investigator in 35.4 percent of patients versus 15.5 percent of controls. Still, 35.4 percent is fewer than half, and a great deal remains to be explored in this area.

Perhaps, some have theorized, the different findings are connected with severity of the illness. Studies testing this hypothesis, however, have shown conflicting results, and no such connection has been established. Others have suggested that the different figures from different groups of lupus patients may be associated with *other* findings in those patients, such as particular antibodies—and here, there seems to be something definite. One study, for example, compared the incidence of two of these factors in lupus patients with or without anti-Ro and anti-nRNP antibodies (see Chapter 3 for a discussion of these and other significant antibodies). In patients with anti-Ro antibodies, B8 was found in 81 percent, DRw3 in 100 percent; in those with anti-nRNP, the figures for the two factors were 29 percent and 33 percent; and in those with neither, they were 41 percent and 25 percent. Another researcher found DRw3 in 70 percent of those with anti-DNA antibodies, in only 37 percent of those without.

It must be added that DRw4, the marker linked with rheumatoid arthritis—and *not* DRw2 or DRw3—has been found associated with *drug-induced* lupus. It must also be added that two of those believed linked with idiopathic lupus, B8 and DRw3, have *also* been found associated with a number of other diseases, including juvenile (insulin-dependent) diabetes mellitus.

In short, the terrain known as the MHC remains in great part *terra incognita*, so far as its role in disease is concerned. As it is further mapped and more of its constituents are identified, more facts will doubtless emerge from what at this writing can only be termed tantalizing hints.

Which brings us to the final facet of the heredity question: mode of inheritance. All of the flatly hereditary disorders we mentioned earlier are recessive, whether X-linked or autosomal—a mechanism that simply would not fit the demographic facts of lupus. Those terms may, for some readers, require a bit of explanation, which will necessarily be brief and somewhat oversimplified.

Each human zygote, or fertilized egg cell, contains 23 pairs of chromosomes, half contributed by the ovum (egg cell) and half by the sperm uniting with that ovum. One pair are the sex chromosomes. Each of a normal female's body cells has two X chromosomes (she is designated XX), and she can contribute only an X to her offspring; a normal male has one X and one Y (XY), and his sperm may carry either. The other 22 pairs of chromosomes are called autosomes.

All the chromosomes carry genes, the units in which hereditary information is encoded, and each trait has its fixed place, technically termed its locus, on a particular chromosome. The emergent trait in a particular individual depends upon the combined information contributed by the genes at corresponding loci on each pair. If information is the same at corresponding loci, the individual is said to be homozygous for the trait in question; if not, the individual is heterozygous for that trait.

A familiar illustration is eye color. An individual who has received genes for blue eyes from both parents is homozygous for eye color and is blue-eyed; similarly, genes for dark eyes from both parents will mean the individual is homozygous for eye color and has dark eyes. Each can pass on only like information to his or her offspring. But someone whose eye-color inheritance is heterozygous—i.e., there is opposite information at the corresponding loci on the particular pair of chromosomes involved—will *not* have eyes of some neutral hue; he or she will have dark eyes. That is because, for certain traits, one message is dominant and will prevail over the opposite, which is termed recessive; eye color is one such trait, and the gene for dark eyes is dominant. An individual heterozygous for a particular trait may pass on *either* piece of genetic information to his or her offspring.†

The "odds" for a particular autosomal trait that behaves in this dominant-recessive manner may be easily calculated, and they are the same for all such traits. We can designate the homozygous individual either DD (in the case of eye color, dark-eyed) or RR (light-eyed), the heterozygous individual DR (dark-eyed). Simply noting the various possible combinations reveals the probabilities:

† Lest readers whose eyes appear neither clearly blue nor clearly dark feel slighted, further comment is perhaps in order. All coloring in the body, of the eyes as well as the skin and hair, depends chiefly upon a brownish pigment called melanin. Apparent color of the iris, which is to a degree translucent, results from the amount and distribution of pigment combined with reflective phenomena, and individual eye structure is also a factor. A small amount of pigment, concentrated in the deepest layer of the iris, will be perceived as blue. While the genetic mechanism is not fully understood, scattered depositions of pigment in upper layers of the iris apparently produce the hues we perceive as gray, green, hazel, etc.—essentially variants of the recessive trait. It should also be noted that the likelihood of two light-eyed persons producing a light-eyed child is actually not 100 percent but an estimated 98 percent; uncommonly, the normally dominant gene for dark eyes seems for unknown reasons to behave in a recessive manner.

| Parental Genes | Possible Combinations | "Odds" for Offspring |
|---|---|---|
| DD+RR | DR only | All heterozygous |
| DD+DR | DD, DD, DR, DR | 50% heterozygous, 50% dominant-homozygous |
| RR+DR | RR, RR, DR, DR | 50% heterozygous, 50% recessive-homozygous |
| DR+DR | DD, DR, DR, RR | 50% heterozygous, 25% dominant-homozygous, 25% recessive-homozygous |

If the recessive trait in question is not light eyes but a disorder, it will be immediately apparent, from the second and fourth situations, how two healthy individuals' genes might combine to produce a child with either the recessive gene or the disorder itself. (It must be noted that the "odds" in the last column prevail anew for each child, just as the outcome of a second flip of a coin is not determined by the outcome of the first.) With a few exceptions, autosomal hereditary disorders *are* recessive; all the well-known ones are, including cystic fibrosis, phenylketonuria (PKU), Tay-Sachs disease, albinism, and the hereditary anemias. In some such disorders, including sickle-cell anemia, the heterozygous individual may display the condition to an extent but in very mild form.

There is no preference displayed for either sex in traits or conditions that follow this straightforward dominant-recessive mode of inheritance. Hence, if it prevails in lupus, there must be some other factor or factors involved, certainly having to do with sex differences per se, and very possibly—as discussed in Chapter 4—with sex hormones.

The other technical term we used earlier is "X-linked." There are quite a few traits, virtually all disorders of one sort or another, dependent upon genes carried on the X chromosome. They are practically all recessive, specifically to a "normal" gene on another X chromosome. Thus, since the normal male is XY and has no "counteracting" gene, the vast majority of those affected by these conditions are males; among X-linked recessive disorders that display this pattern are hemophilia, Fabry's disease, and classic red-green color blindness. Again, as with the autosomal recessives, heterozygous "carriers"—here invariably females—may evidence minimal symptoms of the condition.

Clearly, lupus cannot be of X-linked recessive inheritance. Is there such a thing as X-linked *dominant* inheritance? Yes, there is; it is extremely rare, but a few such conditions have been documented. (None are major disorders. One, for example, involves discoloration of the teeth due to defective enamel.) Following the dominant-recessive pattern, there would be a fifty-fifty chance for an afflicted woman to transmit the gene to her offspring of either sex; an afflicted male would transmit it to all of his daughters but to none of his sons.

Two theories relating to possible X-linked dominant inheritance of lupus have been expressed. One is that such a pattern does prevail but that the gene that might otherwise precipitate the development of lupus in male offspring is "countered" by certain other factors, perhaps by a gene on the normal Y chromosome.

A second theory postulates a constellation of genetic factors: the X-linked dominant (possibly involving more than one gene) *coupled* with autosomal traits, combining to create a congenial climate for the precipitation of lupus by environmental factors or agents.

In the next chapter, we examine the evidence relating to one prominent class of suspected precipitators.

# 6. The Viral Connection

As we have seen, people like to be able to pin down causes for ailments. It makes things, well, neater. That has, of course, been true since the dawn of history. Ills have been ascribed not only to divine displeasure, astrological events, and ill winds (as we saw in the case of syphilis), but to demons, witches, and assorted bad habits.

The culprits sought in our own century are a bit more specific. A number of microscopic organisms have been unequivocally shown to cause a host of human ills from plague to warts. The common cold can confidently be blamed on well over a hundred separate viruses. It follows that such agents are suspected of being behind some of the more complex maladies still frustrating medicine. Lupus is one of them.

By and large, evidence of infection, whether viral or bacterial, may be adduced in two ways. One is by isolating the agent from the patient and clearly identifying it. The second is by demonstrating the existence of antibodies to that organism, which shows evidence of either present or past activity of the agent. (Antibodies, you will recall, are produced by the body only in response to specific antigens.) Those, at least, are the recognized procedures in infections that behave according to the rules—which most infections do. But not all. Or not always: it is now known that some viruses, in particular, may behave in an extremely aberrant manner under some circumstances.

We'll return to the first of those procedures and see how the scientists have fared. Before that, let's look at the second.

Have unusual numbers of antibodies to known infectious agents turned up in lupus patients?

They have—and they appear to be highly specific. As you may imagine, no such agent has been overlooked; investigators have considered, and sought to eliminate, every bacterial, fungal, protozoan, rickettsial, viral, and other kind of organism known to cause disease of any description in human beings. Only one group remains suspect: viruses. And certain types of viruses have been discounted as well.

While some viruses remain unclassified, the great majority have been categorized in various groups according to their size, structure, and other characteristics. There are, for example, the *arboviruses*—short for "arthropod-borne," reflecting the fact that they are transmitted from person to person (or from animal to person) by arthropod vectors such as ticks, mosquitoes, etc.; the ills they cause include equine encephalitis, dengue, yellow fever, and others. None of the arboviruses has been implicated in lupus.

The flu viruses—the well-known A and B strains, plus a related C strain that causes occasional mild infections—are classed as *myxoviruses,* viruses that have a particular affinity for mucous membranes (their name derives from the Greek *myxa,* "mucus"). Lupus patients have *not* been found to have higher antibody levels to these viruses than anyone else.

Likewise, several other viral categories have been exonerated; at least, no evidence has been found that points to their involvement. They include the *herpesviruses,* the ones responsible for cold sores, most canker sores, chicken pox and shingles, and a number of other conditions; the *poxviruses* (the smallpox virus is the most prominent member of this group); the *adenoviruses* (the first part of the word refers to their fondness for lymphoid tissue), which circulate more or less constantly among children—causing a variety of nose, throat, and eye infections—and to which most adults have high levels of antibodies; the *enteroviruses* (normally found in human intestine), which include the polioviruses and others; and some smaller groups.

There have been conflicting reports regarding a group

called *parainfluenza viruses.* There are four known strains of these viruses (characterized simply by number), typically causing simple colds in adults but far more serious respiratory ills—notably croup and bronchopneumonia—in infants. Some researchers have reported unusually high levels, in lupus patients, of antibodies to the parainfluenza viruses in general (that was true of the twin with lupus we talked about in Chapter 5—but not of her sister). One investigation reported high levels only of antibodies to parainfluenza 1; two other studies found lupus patients no different from control groups in that regard but reported significantly higher levels of antibodies to parainfluenza 2. Several subsequent studies have appeared to confirm the significance of parainfluenza 1. The meaning of these contradictory findings is not clear.

(It should be noted that the parainfluenza viruses are quite widespread and that, as with the adenoviruses, antibodies are found in the majority of people. Some of the reported conflicts have hinged upon the differing significance attributed to particular titers by various researchers.)

Earlier, we mentioned enteroviruses. Within that category is a subgroup called *ECHO viruses,* the acronym standing for "enteric cytopathogenic human orphan" viruses; the "orphan" relates to the belief, when these viruses were first identified, that they did not cause any illnesses.* It is now known that the early supposition was untrue. While most of the ills caused by the ECHO viruses are minor, they are major agents of viral meningitis.

That is by way of introduction to the fact that there is a similar group known as *reoviruses,* the first part of the word standing for "respiratory enteric orphan." They were formerly grouped with the ECHO viruses but are now considered a separate class. A number of studies have recorded a significantly high percentage of lupus patients with antibodies to these viruses, in particular the strain known as reovirus 1; one investigation found such antibodies in 55 percent of a

---

* We do not, frankly, know what led to the "orphan" designation, but the word does conjure up a touching picture of a small, helpless, and homeless wanderer, innocently fending for itself as best it can.

group of lupus patients, in a mere 3 percent of an equal number of controls. Reoviruses have occasionally been found in association with mild febrile ills and with bouts of mild diarrhea, but no cause-and-effect relationship has been proved.

The alert reader may be aware that a number of major viral diseases have not been mentioned: measles, for one; mumps, for a second; rubella is a third. The measles and mumps viruses have been classed as *paramyxoviruses* (they are similar to, but larger than, the myxoviruses); the virus that causes rubella has been tentatively placed in this category. And it is here that the most telling data have been reported. Quite a few of the studies of lupus patients have found higher incidence, and higher titers as well, of antibodies to the mumps virus; most reports have cited the rubella virus; and *the measles virus had been listed without exception.*

There are a number of reasons why this fact may be extremely significant. They relate both to hints that have emerged in other research on lupus and to recent revelations and hypotheses regarding two other conditions.

One point is the nature of the suspect virus(es). All viruses are classed generally as either deoxyviruses or riboviruses, according to whether their cores consist of deoxyribonucleic acid (DNA) or ribonucleic acid (RNA). Many of those we listed earlier as believed innocent of any connection with lupus—including the herpesviruses, the poxviruses, and the adenoviruses—are deoxyviruses. The paramyxoviruses (as well as the reoviruses, the parainfluenza viruses, and the myxoviruses) are riboviruses, viruses with RNA cores. As noted in Chapter 3, a marked incidence has been found in lupus patients of antinuclear antibodies to both double-stranded DNA and double-stranded RNA; the latter is a type common in RNA viruses but not in mammalian tissues.

Recently, there has been interest in another group of RNA viruses, called *retroviruses,* and in a particular subclass of them called "type C" viruses or *oncornaviruses.* The "onco" part of that word is from the Greek *onkos,* "mass"; in medical parlance, it denotes something that is tumor-related or, by extension, causes malignant growth of any kind. (Physicians engaged in the treatment of malignancies are *oncologists.*) Such viruses had long been known to exist in various animals; one causes a type of sarcoma in chickens, for example, and another causes leukemia in mice. But until recently, no such virus had been found in association with any illness, malignant or other, in human beings. In 1981, it was announced by the National Cancer Institute that the existence of a human oncornavirus had been confirmed; that virus has been christened HTLV, for "human T-cell leukemia virus," and it causes a rare form of leukemia.

The interest in such viruses vis-à-vis lupus stems from the fact that, in experimental animals, type C viruses have also been found in association with lupuslike disease, in the absence of any malignancies (see Chapter 8). No such virus has yet been found in association with lupus or any other autoimmune disorder in humans—but that does not mean none exists. And it should be added that antibodies to HTLV have been found in a few perfectly healthy people.

That a virus or class of viruses could be connected with more than one type of illness is not particularly startling. The human herpesviruses, for instance, have long been known to do so. These viruses, after causing an initial infection, are wont to linger silently in the body, chiefly in nerve cells, reemerging later to cause recurrent problems—or entirely different ones; herpes simplex viruses type 1 (cold sores) and type 2 (genital herpes) are perhaps the most familiar. Another herpesvirus, the varicella-zoster virus, initially causes chicken pox—and may reappear later to precipitate a case of painful shingles. Still another, the Epstein-Barr virus (EBV), is the perpetrator of mononucleosis; it can also cause recurrent tonsillitis; and it is suspected to be the cause of a tumor called Burkitt's lymphoma (which is rare in the United States but common in some parts of Africa). And EBV, as it happens, has been linked indirectly to another autoimmune disorder, rheumatoid arthritis.

A new sort of antibody was found in a major British study

reported early in 1980, an antibody found in 93 percent of a
series of rheumatoid arthritis patients but in a mere 16 percent of a control group. The antibody is specifically to a
substance, found in certain lymphocytes, which for lack of a
better designation was dubbed "rheumatoid-arthritis-associ-
ated nuclear antigen"—RANA, for short. And there seems to
be a connection with EBV.

By the age of thirty, most Americans have antibodies to
EBV, triggered by prior infection—infection which may
have been so mild that it was never diagnosed. Some of them
also have anti-RANA antibodies, which appear to develop
somewhat later, if they develop at all. No one seems to have
anti-RANA antibodies *without* anti-EBV antibodies. Hence,
the hypothesis that EBV infection somehow sets off another
process in some people, culminating in the appearance of
RANA. The EBV-RANA connection has been confirmed by
U.S. researchers, and one, Dr. Michael A. Catalano of the
Scripps Clinic & Research Foundation in La Jolla, California,
has suggested an interplay with a genetic factor: Perhaps the
development of rheumatoid arthritis, in individuals with
RANA, is contingent upon the presence of the DRw4 factor
noted in Chapter 5 to be associated with the disease.

Needless to say, if further studies absolutely confirm a particular virus as the precipitating factor in rheumatoid arthritis, lupus, or any other autoimmune disease—*and* those at
risk for the disease can be genetically identified—then the
next step will be clear: a vaccine to protect susceptible persons from that virus. Those "ifs" still loom very large, and
such an achievement, while devoutly to be wished for, is
unlikely to take place in the near future. But to return to
viruses and lupus.

We said earlier that one traditional proof of the usual infectious disease is isolation of a specific virus from the patient.
No clearly identified virus has been isolated in lupus. But
something very suggestive of a virus or some form thereof
*has* been found.

The first to describe such findings was Houston's Dr. Fe-
renc Györkey, who in the late 1960s reported isolating mate-

rial he characterized as "myxoviruslike" structures; he and his colleagues suggested in a later report detailing similar findings that these appeared to be "subviral structures" rather than entire viruses. It has been confirmed that the structures consist of RNA.

Since Dr. Györkey's initial announcement, a number of other investigators have pursued the same avenue of research, with the same results. All have described the structures or particles as "myxoviruslike" or "paramyxoviruslike." They have been found in the kidneys, skin, white cells, nerve cells, and other tissues of lupus patients. (It is notable that at least one reported instance involved a kidney transplant. The mysterious particles had been found in the patient's own kidneys. At the time of surgery, the new kidney was proved virus free. One month later, biopsy of the new kidney revealed identical particles.) A few researchers have reported finding them in isolated cases of other rheumatic diseases. They have *not* been isolated from any healthy controls.

If the measles virus or another RNA virus is in fact implicated in lupus, it is certainly not via the viral mechanisms with which we are familiar.

Some have theorized that the situation might be compared to the behavior of the herpesviruses, with the viral agent causing one condition early on, and lupus later. But with the herpesviruses, the virus can be isolated in its later reappearance(s). Further, it remains communicable; some chicken-pox epidemics have, in fact, been launched by a child's exposure to an adult with shingles. Lupus is, of course, not contagious.

It is more likely that explanation of the phenomenon— assuming the postulated viral connection does exist—lies in another direction: the etiology that has come to be known as the *slow virus*. Most of the handful of conditions traced to such a mechanism are limited to isolated exotic climes or are of decreasing epidemiological interest (parkinsonism, one of the latter, afflicts no one born after the 1930s, and the virus originally responsible—it may have been a variant of the influenza virus, which mutates constantly—apparently no longer exists). Two, however, are of continuing interest, particularly in connection with the research we have detailed in this chapter.

One is Dawson's encephalitis or subacute sclerosing panencephalitis, known to physicians and lay persons alike simply as SSPE. It is an illness that involves insidious, gradual deterioration of the brain, with concomitant neuromuscular, sensory, and mental disintegration; its victims are typically between the ages of five and twenty, three quarters of them boys (the reason for the gender imbalance is still unknown). There is no treatment, and death is inevitable. Thirty to fifty new U.S. cases have been reported annually in recent years; it is believed that there may be twice that number.

Early on, research in SSPE had revealed strange structures or particles in brain tissue—structures described as "myxoviruslike." Later, as suspicion of viral etiology grew, antibodies were investigated; markedly elevated titers of antimeasles antibody were found in SSPE patients. Finally, in 1970, measles virus itself was isolated from the brains of victims, and it was established that SSPE is, in fact, due to apparent reactivation of that virus—"smoldering," meanwhile, in both central-nervous-system and lymph tissues—in a child who has had measles.

Of course, most children who have had measles do not later fall victim to SSPE. (A measles vaccine was introduced in 1963, but it was not established until recently that immunization before the age of fifteen months does not provide reliable protection. With increased public awareness of that fact, care on the part of parents and physicians to see that children are properly vaccinated, and—it is hoped—decline of measles itself, the incidence of SSPE, which has declined markedly since the 1960s, will continue to decline as well.) It is evident that some agent or factor must account for its selectivity, some factor that "awakens" the virus (or permits it to remain in the first place). Aside from the sex imbalance, SSPE is known to be most prevalent in the Southeast. And one major study has found a history, in a significant number of SSPE cases, of contact with a dog suffering from canine distemper—which, perhaps entirely coincidentally, is caused by an RNA virus.

The other condition in which parallels with lupus, as well as with SSPE, can be drawn is multiple sclerosis (MS).

Some 250,000 Americans are believed afflicted by multiple sclerosis. Like SSPE, it is more prevalent in one part of the country—but in the North rather than in the South (it is some forty times more common in Minnesota, for example, than in Mexico City).† Like SSPE, it affects the nervous system. Unlike SSPE, but like lupus, it is chronic and may have no particular effect on life expectancy. And there are a number of other similarities to lupus, as well.

Like lupus, MS typically strikes between the ages of fifteen and forty (although there is no particular sex preference). The primary kind of lesion is demyelinization (disintegration of the sheath surrounding nerves and its replacement by scar tissue), a phenomenon that, while not predominant, is sometimes seen in lupus. As in lupus: familial "clusters" have been reported; the condition may be aggravated by extremes of heat or cold; a relapse-and-remission pattern is frequent; there has been some therapeutic success with corticosteroids (though not to the degree seen in lupus); association with certain histocompatability factors (see Chapter 5) has been observed, notably—there seems to be a geographical variance—with DRw2 and DRw4. There have, further, been at least eight cases reported in which laboratory findings suggested lupus—while the clinical picture was that of typical

† On a worldwide basis, MS is most prevalent in two broad bands that encircle the globe both north and south; these are basically the cool temperate areas, from approximately 40° to 60° latitude. A study reported in late 1976 revealed an interesting sidelight. In that investigation, a group of British researchers explored the effects of migration to or from such areas of statistically higher "risk" upon the actual incidence of MS. The age of fifteen appears, from the results, to be a significant one. Among those emigrating from Great Britain, a "high risk" area, to a "low risk" locale after the age of fifteen, the incidence of MS proved no different from that prevailing in England; conversely, immigrants to Great Britain from "low risk" parts of the world after that age are still at lower "risk." And those in the latter group whose parents had also been born in "low risk" areas showed a still lower MS incidence—strongly suggesting the possibility of genetic as well as environmental factors, at least in susceptibility.

MS. Like lupus, MS is often referred to as an "autoimmune" disorder. (Some have tentatively wondered if some cases of MS—even, perhaps, all cases of MS—represent a special form of lupus.)

Many researchers have found unusually high levels of antibodies to measles virus in MS patients. And in late 1975, Drs. Gertrude and Werner Henle and Drs. Paul and Ursula Koldovsky of Philadelphia confirmed the existence of a "viruslike" agent in the brain and sera of MS patients; others have since reported "myxoviruslike" or "paramyxoviruslike" fragments in MS patients, as well as what appeared to be genetic material from herpes simplex virus.

Both SSPE and MS have been investigated primarily by neurological researchers. With the establishment of a "slow virus" etiology for the former, there is strong suspicion in neurological circles of such an etiology in MS as well.

Viruses are essentially parasitic organisms; they are dependent upon living cellular material for their survival and propagation (hence are more difficult to study than such organisms as bacteria, which can be grown in broths and other nutrients in the laboratory—while viruses require live animals, fertilized eggs, or tissue cultures). Normally, in a process called replication, a virus attaches itself to the host cell at predetermined receptor sites, penetrates the cell, and loses its outer coat, releasing nuclear material (DNA or RNA, as the case may be); it then reassembles and is released by the cell— now infectious, but also now vulnerable to the host's defense mechanisms. That is what happens in an ordinary infection. That is *not* what happens when a virus becomes a "slow" virus, reappearing years later in altered guise to set off not an acute, contagious infection but a noncontagious condition either chronic or acute.

One theory that has been put forth, specifically relating to multiple sclerosis but possibly relating to lupus as well, is that, for some reason, the host cells fail to release the virus following replication. The theory postulates that the presence of the virus stimulates the formation of antibodies but that those antibodies are unable to attack the virus, because it still remains hidden within the body's cells. Thus, the antibodies attack what is available: the cells of the host.

(It should also be mentioned that the paramyxoviruses require an enzyme, produced by the host, for activation. Thus, it has been postulated that if the required enzyme is lacking —a deficiency that has not been specifically pinpointed in any of the disorders we've mentioned—the virus might simply linger an abnormally long time within the cell, causing damage to the host cell itself.)

Dr. Charles L. Christian, a distinguished researcher associated with Cornell University Medical College, has pointed out that whatever the virus (if there is a virus involved), it is clear that antigens stimulating the production of antibodies (and inflammation) evidently persist. He has suggested the possibility that the virus, persisting within the host cell, alters the cell in such a way that some constituents of the cell are no longer recognized as belonging to the host by the immune-defense mechanisms—and "become," in that sense, "foreign" antigens. That may lead, in turn, to the fight-the-foreign-substance activities that cause the inflammation seen in lupus.

It is known that genes of the "slow" viruses are capable of actually integrating themselves into the genes of human cells. Moscow's Dr. V. M. Zhdanov established in 1974 that the measles virus is capable of that sort of activity. In 1975, Dr. Zhdanov reported that he had found nuclear material derived from the genes of the measles virus in the genes of a number of lupus patients—but not, significantly, in a group of controls. Dr. Zhdanov's intriguing theory is that the virus somehow integrates its genes into the genes of the victim's cells; the genes then produce a variety of new proteins, which proceed to incorporate themselves into the host cell membranes. There they act as antigens—biochemically "fooling" the body and its defense mechanisms into viewing them as foreign matter and initiating the inflammatory process.

Any, or none, of these theories may be correct, but the case for an infectious, and probably viral, connection is a strong one. As Dr. Christian put it at a fall 1981 symposium on lupus co-sponsored by the National Kidney Foundation and the American Rheumatism Association, such an agent may well be the "trigger puller" in a situation in which host factors—including both sex and genetic variables—provide some of the ammunition and weaponry. He feels that "an atypical microorganism, such as a retrovirus, deserves consideration, but the common and typical viruses are more promising candidates."

Noting the great variety of lupus manifestations, he also pointed out a parallel with the hepatitis B virus (hepatitis B, once erroneously believed transmissible only directly into the bloodstream, was previously known as "serum hepatitis"). The response to infection by this virus is extremely variable and may include not only liver inflammation (which may be either acute or chronic) but acute arthritis, neuritis, dermatitis, chronic kidney inflammation—and/or polyarteritis. Polyarteritis nodosa ("inflammation of many arteries" accompanied by the formation of nodules) is an autoimmune disorder afflicting chiefly men in their middle years; antibodies to hepatitis B virus can be found in at least 25 percent, and perhaps as many as 50 percent, of polyarteritis nodosa patients.

In any case, whatever the "trigger puller," the rest of the clues to the crime may be found within the extraordinarily complex network of normally defensive weaponry called the immune system.

# 7. B Cells, T Cells, and Forbidden Clones

Certainly the most mysterious aspect of lupus is that phenomenon called autoimmunity—mobilization of the body's defense system against the body itself. Not only do lupus patients evidence higher-than-normal antibody levels against particular viruses; they also evidence antibodies that can be clearly shown to be specifically primed for battle against the body's own tissues—against the patient's own red cells, blood vessels, muscles, and other organs.

It is not completely clear, as yet, precisely how the tissue damage that is evident in lupus takes place. In Chapter 3, we mentioned "pockets of activity," units of antibody locked in combat with antigen, which draw complement to the battle scene. These units are called *immune complexes*. They can be found in heavy concentration in inflamed tissues. They can also be found circulating in the bloodstream, especially when the disease is active. When serum from such patients is chilled, a precipitate sometimes emerges, termed cryoglobulin (from the Greek *kryos*, "cold"); it does so because it is less soluble at lower temperatures. It has now been established that this precipitate consists largely of immune complexes.

One might suppose that antibody, having locked on to the antigen it perceives as the enemy, is not about to stir up any further trouble. That may not be so; immune complexes may themselves cause tissue damage in some way—perhaps by irritating those tissues or perhaps, it has been speculated, by triggering some sort of toxic reaction. But whether it is autoantibodies, or the resultant immune complexes, or both which are responsible for the actual tissue destruction in lupus, something is unquestionably awry at a very basic immune-system level. One might say, in computer terms, that the hardware is malfunctioning—but that malfunction stems directly from a problem with the software, some serious error in the "programming" of the immune system.

The immune system revolves especially around a subgroup of the leukocytes, or white cells, called lymphocytes. Production of these cells begins very early, in the embryonic yolk; it continues in the fetal liver; after birth, it is centered in the thymus gland and in bone marrow. This initial activity produces, actually, immature cells called *stem cells* or *precursor cells,* essentially defenders-to-be not yet differentiated as to function. Differentiation takes place during maturation of the cells.

Some mature in the thymus and emerge as distinct entities known as T (for "thymus-dependent") cells; others mature in the bone marrow and emerge as B (for "bone-marrow-derived") cells. Both types proceed, as mature, competent lymphocytes, to their stations throughout the body: the lymph nodes, the blood, the spleen, and various tissues and ducts situated primarily in the thorax.

T cells participate prominently in cell-mediated immune responses, interacting directly with antigens. They apparently constitute the body's first line of defense against a number of microorganisms, including many bacteria and most viruses; recent studies strongly suggest that they also play a leading role in transplant rejection and in a "surveillance" system that guards against potential malignancies.

B cells give rise to plasma cells and effect antibody responses via the production of immunoglobulins. They are believed to play the major role in repelling incursions by coccal bacteria, a few of the viruses, and certain toxins.

As we have emphasized, these defenses are brought into play against specific provoking agents or antigens, which must first be encountered in order that the process be initiated. An antigen may be defined as a chemical "flag" carried by the invading cell (be it that of a bacterium, a virus, a poisonous substance, or transplanted tissue) that identifies it as not belonging, not self. What normally happens is roughly as follows. (As in Chapter 5, we have here highly simplified what is in fact an extremely complex biochemical process.)

Upon encounter with a specific antigen, the lymphocytes respond in a predetermined manner. A few cells of both types are altered, become replicating lymphoblasts, and undergo a series of divisions that produce, in the end, groups of identical "daughter cells" equipped to repel that particular antigen.

The B cells' daughters, or "effectors," are plasma cells coded to produce specific immunoglobulins. The new T cells release substances called lymphokines, which include chemicals that can kill or otherwise disable the antigen-bearing target cells. (Some twenty lymphokines have been identified, although the specific functions of all of them are not known. One is interferon, an antiviral protein. Another is lymphotoxin, which is "poisonous" to the invading antigen. A third is MIF, for "migration inhibition factor," which apparently attempts to localize the reaction by drawing macrophages to the vicinity and keeping them there. Macrophages are large phagocytes, a word derived from the Greek and literally meaning "eating cells"; phagocytes are white cells that function more or less as cleanup crews, ingesting dead or incapacitated cells, including those of pathogenic organisms and other foreign material as well as worn-out cells discarded by the body itself in the normal course of events.) The lymphokines have recently attracted special interest on the research front, and we shall return to them.

Some of the T cells also function as "helpers" in the B cells' operations. And some daughter cells of both types are modified, coded or "programmed" to "remember" that antigen and to immediately respond in a similar manner upon subsequent encounter with it.

Inflammation is the evidence of this defensive process, whether it appears in the throat in response to a streptococcal infection, in the nose when tissues there are attacked by a virus, or in the skin surrounding a splinter. The immune system and its activities are necessary to life; were it not for them, we would succumb shortly after birth to the host of inimical agents and substances in our environment. Indeed, some children, victims of the uncommon congenital conditions called immune deficiency diseases, are at just such risk and must receive regular injections of immunoglobulins or be kept in isolated, completely sterile environments. (There are several such conditions, of varying degree and severity. The most serious one follows a classic X-linked mode of inheritance and affects chiefly boys.) The "A" in AIDS—for *acquired* immune deficiency syndrome—specifically distinguishes that disorder from the congenital type.

The situation in lupus is precisely the reverse. Not a deficiency but a surfeit of immunoglobulins causes the problem. Further, the lupus patient's lymphocytes appear to act indiscriminately, staging attacks not only against foreign invaders but against her own tissues and organs. One might, in fact, describe their actions as deliberately discriminatory, singling out such tissues for their punishing activity. Why does this happen? Or, conversely, why *doesn't* it occur in the vast majority of individuals?

It must be emphasized at this point that the foregoing description of the immune-response process is based on observations to date—but that the entire area is under continuing investigation; very little was known or understood concerning these mechanisms until the past few years. What follows is in large part speculation.

To begin with, remember that the lymphocytes' actions are initiated only by encounter with specific antigens. Normally, an individual's lymphocytes are evidently programmed to ignore the body's own antigens—cell-surface "flags" that communicate an "I belong here" message; only cells that do not belong, those with potential for compromising the integrity of the body, are singled out for destruction. The former kinds of cells are let alone, tolerated; the latter are not tolerated and are attacked.

Intolerance is another word for allergy. There are some

substances that are inherently harmless to the human body and are so perceived by most of those bodies. When an individual exhibits an unusual inflammatory reaction to a substance—whether it be a pollen, a food, or a medication—we say that individual is allergic to that substance. As we have noted, lupus patients appear to have a heavier incidence of such allergies than other people. Typical of the investigations that have provided such data was one conducted at Johns Hopkins University in 1973; 26 percent of a group of lupus patients, versus 10 percent of a control group, reported a history of hives; 35 percent of the lupus group, but only 20 percent of the controls, reported a history of drug allergy (often in the lupus group, but not among the controls, manifested by arthritic symptoms). We don't know what this might imply.

And lupus patients appear to be, in a sense, also "allergic" to their own tissues.

A number of theories have been suggested to explain this anomaly.

One such theory, that of "sequestered antigens," postulates that some chemical substances occurring naturally within the body may somehow be hidden away during early embryonic development, while the lymphocyte-producing organs are "learning" to recognize the individual's own cellular material and developing "tolerance" to it. Later, when these substances are released into the circulation from wherever they have been sequestered, they encounter mature lymphocytes which fail to recognize them and thus behave exactly as if they were entirely foreign antigens. Since no one has demonstrated an antenatal cache of hidden antigens, this hypothesis does not appear to be the likely answer.

Another speculation, which might be called the "shotgun" theory, holds that the immune response in autoimmune disease might actually be directed at a truly foreign antigen (perhaps a virus) and that some of the body's own tissues fall victim as well. This theory might in fact explain rheumatic fever, which has long been considered a hypersensitive or "allergic" reaction to streptococcal infection; in more than half of all rheumatic fever patients, there has been found an antibody to streptococci that also reacts to myocardial (heart-muscle) tissue (the condition is sometimes called "autoimmune carditis").

The question of course arises as to why the defender cells lack the ability to distinguish between the invader and the native tissue; a heart-muscle cell is quite different from a bacterium. One possible explanation is that the native tissue has been altered in some way, conceivably by a bacterium, virus, or other pathogenic organism, so that its antigenic identification is blurred; such a phenomenon, involving a virus, has indeed been suggested in relation to both multiple sclerosis and lupus (see Chapter 6).

If the native tissue has not been biochemically altered, then it must be assumed that something has gone awry in the immune-response process. (The two possibilities are not, of course, mutually exclusive.) Which brings us to the last part of our chapter title: the "forbidden clone"—and confirmation of what was presented as pure speculation in the first edition of this book.

Part of the initial immune reaction we described earlier consists of cloning—replication of a generation of identical daughter cells by a lymphocyte. It is possible that occasionally, in everyone, an aberrant lymphocyte arises, one that is capable of taking destructive action against that individual's own tissues. For the body's own health and survival, this is not a good thing. Therefore, it was postulated, there must be a built-in "control mechanism" that normally eliminates such randomly arising cells or inhibits their action, "precensors" them and prevents their generating a "forbidden clone," a group of cells capable of constitutional injury.

In lupus and other autoimmune disorders, the self-protective mechanism fails to function: the randomly emerging, erroneously "keyed" lymphocyte, uncensored, does proceed to replicate, and produces what should not be: the forbidden clone. Those who put forth this theory suggested that the renegade lymphocytes are B cells, and that the T cells may—in addition to acting as "helpers" and "instructors"—have a "suppressor" function that halts inappropriate B-cell behavior; the forbidden clone thus suggests T-cell deficiency. Since the forbidden clone is presumably generated in the same manner as an approved clone, there would also be daughter cells "memory"-coded to go into similar action every time the antigen is encountered—a frequent occurrence when the antigen in question is a part of the body itself.

The thymus, the endocrine gland responsible for the T cells, also produces a substance, tentatively classed as a hormone, that has been named thymosin. While the relationship of this substance to T-cell maturation is unclear, thymosin has been extracted from calf thymus and used successfully to treat congenital lack of immunity associated with underdevelopment of the gland, presumably based on a deficiency of "helper" T cells. Unusually low levels of thymosin activity have been detected in some lupus patients—although it is not yet known exactly what this may mean in terms of the cause or course of the disease.

A great deal is known now, and was not known just a few years ago, about the nature and activity of B cells and T cells, both normally and in lupus.

It is now known that the culprits *are* the B cells—and that in lupus patients, even when the disease is quiescent, there is an eight- to ten-fold increase in the proliferation of B cells, and they are also unusually active; this activity increases at times of flare-up. It is now known, too, that the postulated "helper" and "suppressor" T cells *do* exist—and that in lupus, there is a marked deficiency of the latter, as well as of the precursor T cells. (In AIDS, as might be expected, precisely the reverse is true; there is a marked deficiency in *helper* T cells.) Levels of helper cells, which produce a substance called "B-cell growth factor," are perfectly normal in lupus patients. Thus, while those helper cells are going about their usual business, encouraging the B cells' behavior—*delinquent* behavior, in this situation—the "police force" of suppressor T cells, which normally constrains that behavior, is distinctly understaffed. It appears, in fact, that among the antibodies produced by the rampaging B cells are antibodies directed specifically against those precursor T cells which are in the process of developing into suppressors; anti-nRNP antibody is believed to be the chief villain. (It has even been demonstrated in the laboratory that serum from lupus patients can inhibit this process in cells from healthy controls.)

That brings us to the new interest in lymphokines we mentioned earlier, three of them in particular. It was once supposed that these proteins produced by lymphocytes were simply part of the armamentarium against viruses and other invaders. Now, on the basis of intensive study by scientists at the National Institutes of Health and elsewhere (study made possible in great part by technological breakthroughs permitting preparation of the proteins in the laboratory), it is known that certain of them function, as well, as intercellular messengers.

One of the lymphokines that have enjoyed special attention, as many readers may be aware, is *interferon*. This antiviral protein may have anticancer effects as well, and there have been well-publicized trials of the substance as possible treatment for both viral infections and various malignancies. Those trials, at this writing, have not been particularly successful. The reason, as reported by a team of Upjohn Company researchers at the October 1983 Interscience Conference on Antimicrobial Agents and Chemotherapy, sponsored by the American Society for Microbiology, may be that a lot of interferon may be too much of a good thing.

In human trials, increasingly high doses of interferon have been used, on the theory that if a little is helpful, a great deal ought to be more so. But Dr. Harold E. Renis and his colleagues at Upjohn, using an interferon inducer (a substance triggering interferon production by the body itself) in laboratory mice, found just the opposite.

Animals given high doses of the inducer, they reported, were thirty-five times less able to fight off a viral invader (the agent used was herpes simplex type 1, the cold-sore virus) than totally untreated animals. Those given low doses, on the other hand, were thirty times better able to withstand the infection than the animals given none. In fact, the high doses had apparently *lowered* the animals' internal production of interferon to a tenth of normal, while the lower doses had boosted it as much as twenty-fold. Other researchers, administering interferon itself to experimental animals, have reported similar effects. A feedback mechanism seems to operate in which high blood levels of interferon may signal T cells to call a halt to further production of the substance.

Interferon also plays another role in the immune process: it stimulates certain activities of macrophages which, in turn, enhance the response to a particular antigen by encouraging the T cells to produce more of the substances lethal to cells carrying the antigen.

Among factors stimulating the production of interferon is another lymphokine, *interleukin-2* (IL2), also called "T-cell growth factor" because its primary function is stimulating the proliferation of T cells in the presence of an antigen. It is IL2, it is believed, which encourages T cells' production of B-cell growth factor. And the release of interleukin-2, in turn, is stimulated by still another substance, called *interleukin-1* (IL1). This substance is also classed as a lymphokine, although it is apparently produced not only by T cells but by macrophages and other cells as well. IL1 is needed for B-cell proliferation, too, since B-cell growth factor acts only in conjunction with it. IL1 also acts on tissues other than lymphocytes.

There appears, in short, to be a continuous exchange of information via an intercellular communications network.

What has all this to do with lupus? For one thing, unusually high interferon levels have been found in lupus patients. For another, T cells from lupus patients produce unusually low quantities of IL2—a seeming paradox, since IL2 stimulates the interferon production. But other factors may well encourage high interferon levels. And the lower-than-normal IL2 does correlate with the T-cell deficit found in lupus. Further, whatever the specific effects of each of these departures from normal, the result is an imbalance in lymphokines considered as a whole.

In another area of medicine, the study of trace elements

(minerals nutritionally required in very small amounts), it has been found that a deficiency of one can create a relative surfeit of another—a situation that can demonstrably lead to trouble. If lupus patients produce lower-than-normal levels of IL2, or any other lymphokine, they may then have higher levels of IL1, proportionally speaking.

IL1, as we noted, acts on tissues other than lymphocytes. It also stimulates the proliferation of fibroblasts, cells that form fibrous tissue at cites of chronic inflammation—and it promotes the production by those cells of certain enzymes, including collagenase, which is a factor in the degradation of connective tissue. It has been found, too, to trigger fever in experimental animals.

And IL1 may play a key role in the arthritis that is typically part of lupus. It acts directly on the synovium, the enveloping membrane of a joint, causing the synovial cells to release both collagenase and inflammation-triggering prostaglandins (a group of substances further discussed in the next chapter).

All of this increasing familiarity with the B cells, T cells, and other elements of the immune system does not tell us what sets off the imbalances—or, possibly, misfiring of intercellular signals—in the first place; that may be a virus, some other environmental agent, hormonal action, or, probably, a combination of factors. Much of what has been learned in these areas has stemmed from research over the years with animal strains that have provided near-perfect laboratory "models" of lupus. Continuing research with those models may bring further clues not only to what happens in lupus but what *makes* it happen.

# 8. The Model Mice

Much of what medicine would like to know about lupus—or any malady, for that matter—is inaccessible. It's true that more and more sophisticated diagnostic and analytic techniques have revealed a wealth of information, and that cautious use of new therapies has immeasurably improved the outlook for patients.

But there are potentially informative and/or beneficial techniques that simply would not be carried out on a human being, because they would be unthinkable. Human patients are not given massive doses of new drugs with totally unknown effects. They are not castrated or relieved of other glands or organs to observe the effects, if any, on their illness. They are not subjected to potentially lethal injections of pathogenic organisms or carcinogenic substances in order to challenge the competence of their immune systems. They are not condemned to diets known to be nutritionally inadequate. They are not forcibly mated with others of their species, inluding close relatives. They are not executed at various ages and stages so that their organs might be laid out on an autopsy table.

These things *can* be done with laboratory animals. It is thus fortunate when a condition similar to a human ailment can be created in an experimental animal (preferably, of course, one which does not represent an endangered species), providing a convenient subject for study and for therapeutic trials. Just such a situation has been extremely helpful, for example, in rheumatoid arthritis: inflammation experimentally induced in the joints of laboratory animals has resulted in much useful information, of direct benefit to arthritis patients, regarding the effects of rest, of physical stress, and of the administration of various anti-inflammatory drugs.

It is even more fortunate when a "model" is found—a particular animal that *naturally* develops a disorder paralleling a human ill. That fortuitous circumstance has occurred in lupus.

In 1959, it was reported by Drs. M. Bielchowsky, B. J. Helyer, and J. B. Howie that a strain of black mice native to New Zealand appeared to develop autoimmune hemolytic anemia spontaneously. This disorder, in which antibodies are formed against the individual's own red blood cells, also occurs in human lupus. Subsequent studies confirmed that the anemia afflicting the mice was also characterized by increased immunoglobulins, proteinuria, and nephritis involving the deposition of antigen-antibody complexes. All animals of this strain are subject to the disorder.

Genetic studies of that strain and others were begun. Many hybrids were produced, displaying many variations of disease. Drs. Helyer and Howie soon determined that crossbreeding the New Zealand black (NZB) mice with a white (NZW) strain resulted in a hybrid that naturally developed an ailment even more striking in its resemblance to systemic lupus—and with invariable occurrence of the serious kidney damage that afflicts as many as half the victims of lupus.

Both the NZB mice and the NZB/NZW hybrids have since been under intensive study in laboratories around the world. The findings and observations that have thus far emerged bear uncanny resemblances to many of the data and theories detailed in the foregoing chapters.

The mice do not develop joint problems. Nor do they exhibit skin lesions, even if induction of such lesions is attempted by clipping or shaving their hair and exposing them to strong ultraviolet light for long periods. But other facets of their disorders are clearly relevant.

The NZB mice develop their disease by the age of twelve to fifteen months (the normal lifespan of an ordinary mouse is up to three years), although some become ill as early as three months of age. Antierythrocyte antibody is produced, and it is strictly a self-destructive agent: it will attack the erythrocytes of other mice (and of rats to a very slight degree) but not the blood of other animals or of humans. The result is a severe anemia that appears within weeks, with progressive weight loss. The anemia is most severe, curiously, in virgin females; in female mice that have been bred, it is statistically a little less severe than in males (although individual animals do show differences from these general pictures).

Some of the NZB mice prove to have antinuclear antibodies and some do not, but there are significantly increased levels of immunoglobulins, in particular IgG and IgM. There is also a high incidence of peptic ulcers (suggesting, possibly, antibody that reacts to the animals' intestinal mucosa), which afflict nearly every animal eventually if it lives beyond the age of two years.

In the NZB/NZW hybrids, it is severe kidney deterioration that predominates, and the damage seen is very much like that which can occur in lupus, primarily involving the glomeruli, the kidney's filtering units. The syndrome usually starts between the ages of six and twelve months (two to six months earlier in females than in males); it becomes in a few short weeks very much like a long-standing, particularly severe, and totally untreated case of human lupus. Titers of antinuclear antibodies rise quickly. The kidneys lose their function very rapidly: seven eighths of the mice die of uremia within six months—and since the disease process begins earlier in the females, their lives are cut even shorter; 90 percent of the females die before they are thirteen months old.

Antibody against double-stranded RNA is found in a majority of the hybrids, as is antibody against DNA; the latter appears to parallel the severity of the renal disease and is present earlier and more often in the females than in the males. (A few of the males, for reasons unknown, seem to "stabilize"; although they eventually succumb to the disease, their condition remains at a chronic "plateau" for a time, rather than plunging downhill.) There are also an accompanying anemia and deficiencies, as in lupus, of the various types of blood cells.

All the factors cited in Chapters 4 through 7 as key clues to the cause of lupus are operative in the model mice as well.

As we've said, in both strains the females are the more severely afflicted. Whether the sex hormones play a part is still an open question. Dr. Norman Talal of the University of California at San Francisco has reported that if NZB males are castrated at the age of two weeks, their disease pattern tends to reflect that of the females—suggesting that the male hormones play a protective role. Spaying of female NZB mice results in decreased production of anti-RNA antibodies, although there is no effect on levels of antibodies against DNA, and no effect on the progress of the disease. If the thymus gland of either sex is removed, the effects are those of gonad removal. Dr. Talal's conclusion: there is some action of the sex hormones on the thymus that affects antibody production.

Some other investigators, however, have tried similar tactics in the NZB/NZW hybrids—castrating or spaying, and then administering hormones of the opposite sex—and have reported that in neither sex is the disease pattern modified in the direction of the other's.

There is absolutely no question, of course, about familial factors in the mice; their disorders are clearly congenital. It is also clear that transmission is genetic rather than transplacental: if fertilized ova from disease-free mice are transferred to the uteruses of NZB mice for gestation, the offspring are perfectly healthy and do not develop any autoimmune disease.

The inheritance pattern appears dominant, since all the mice of these strains are affected. It is not classically sex-linked; hybrids are affected whether the mother is NZB and the father NZW, or vice versa. There is, however, a somewhat different pattern of disease in these two situations: offspring survive longer when the mother is NZB and the father NZW than when the crossbreeding is reversed. Further, the differences affect offspring differently depending upon their

sex. Male offspring of an NZB mother and NZW father survive an average sixty-eight days longer than sons of an NZB
father and NZW mother; some of the former have been
known to live as long as thirty months. In females the average survival difference between the two types of parentage is
only twenty days—which still represents a radically curtailed
lifespan, since all female offspring of NZB fathers and NZW
mothers are dead by the age of sixteen months. These differences remain unexplained.

It has, at any rate, become clear that the mode of inheritance follows no known classic pattern. The short lives of the
model mice have permitted extensive crossbreeding among
the two original strains and various hybrids; none of this has
clarified matters. It is generally believed that whatever the
pattern, several different genes are involved rather than a
single one.

That there is a viral factor is also deemed highly probable.
It has been demonstrated that there is at least one virus
*associated* with the disorder, although a *causal* relationship
has not been established.

There is a group of viruses, apparently distributed
throughout the animal kingdom, that have been labeled
"C types" because in some instances they are known to cause
cancers. They are technically known as oncornaviruses
("onco" for cancer-related, plus RNA; see the discussion of
types of viruses in Chapter 6). Such viruses have been identified in reptiles, birds, and several mammals including mice,
cats, and monkeys. They are evidently species-specific; that
is, each such virus has been isolated only from a single species
of animal. They do not always cause malignant disease; in
fact, they usually do not, and under normal circumstances
their carcinogenic activity is apparently held in check by an
automatic mechanism in the host.

Unlike other viruses, the C viruses are transmitted from
parents to offspring and are thus present from birth. Antibodies to such viruses have been found in the model mice by
many investigators, and particles suggestive of such viruses
have been found in their spleens, kidneys, livers, bone mar-

rows, and a number of other organs. As in human lupus, there have been suggestions that antibodies initially aimed at the viruses are "misdirected" to attack native tissues as well, possibly because the latter have been altered in some way by the virus and release material perceived as a "foreign" antigen. It might be added that the malignancies known to be caused by C viruses are usually lymphomas, involving overproduction of lymphocytes by the spleen and lymph nodes.

Dr. Jay Levy and his colleagues at the University of California at San Francisco have shown that a specific C virus is transmitted—not only in the model mice but in all other strains of house mice they checked—within the egg and sperm cells, meaning that the viral genes must be incorporated with those of the host. This particular virus, interestingly, cannot infect mouse cells—but *can* infect cells of other animals. Dr. Levy dubbed the virus "xenotropic" ("foreign-material-attracted," from the Greek *xenos,* "stranger").

He theorized, from the fact that the virus is found ubiquitously in mice (although the NZB strain has a bit more of it than others), that the virus is normally harmless and possibly even helpful at some stage of embryonic development. And he suggested that some genetic defect in the model mice gives rise to autoimmune disease—whether because inordinate quantities of virus stimulate antibody production or because in these mice the virus alters native cell antigens so that they are no longer recognized as "self."

(As noted in Chapter 6, only one oncornavirus has been found in humans—in association with a rare type of leukemia, and *not* with any autoimmune disorder. It, too, could conceivably be xenotropic, with the primary reservoir in some other species.)

Certainly, as in human lupus, there is some defect of the immune systems of these experimental animals—and again, interest has focused on the distinct roles played by the two different types of lymphocytes, the B and T cells.

It has been shown by several investigators that in these mice, as in human lupus, there is a deficit of the suppressor T cells that control B-cell activity and prevent overproduction by the latter of inappropriate immunoglobulins. This suppressor activity lessens in all mice as they age, and there is a small amount of autoimmune activity in elderly mice just as there is in elderly people. The model mice appear to reach this stage quite prematurely, and the autoimmune activity is of course not minimal but massive. But in these animals, there is some evidence that the B-cell proliferation also is triggered by some other factor—that it is not wholly dependent on the suppressor-T-cell deficit.

The proportions of the two types of cells in the blood, spleen, lymph nodes, etc., of the model mice are normal. But both the NZB mice and the hybrids display structural abnormalities in their thymus glands—which, you will recall, is where T cells mature. An NZB or NZB/NZW thymus transplanted to a normal mouse (after removal of that mouse's own thymus) can actually induce autoimmune disease, proving that there is *something* about the abnormal gland that is involved in the etiology of the disorder.

High levels of immunoglobulins—which are elaborated by the B cells—are, as we mentioned earlier, found in the model mice. Deposits of immunoglobulins (especially IgG), described by investigators as "lumpy," have also been found in their damaged kidneys.

These extra immunoglobulins, however, do *not* confer extra resistance to attack by other organisms. The young model mice are capable of resisting such attack. But that capability diminishes rapidly, and it has severely deteriorated by the time the autoimmune disease has set in—a process demonstrated by viral challenge at various stages. It thus seems that in these animals a population of competent lymphocytes has been diverted from their normal defensive functions into full-time autoantibody production.

The New Zealand mice have been under study for twenty-five years. Now these models have been joined by two others.

In the late 1970s, Edwin Murphy and John Roths of Jackson Laboratories described two more mouse strains which develop lupuslike disease, designated MRL/1 and BXSB. The strains did not evolve naturally but had been bred for other characteristics in unrelated research. Quite unexpectedly, both strains were found to develop lupus spontaneously—as in the New Zealand mice, a heritable disease that affects all animals of the strain. The MRL/1 and BXSB diseases have a great deal in common with the NZB and NZB/NZW picture —but studies to date have revealed some significant differences, as well.

The disease is most acute in the MRL/1 mice. Both males and females fall ill by the age of three or four months, and there is a 90 percent mortality rate in females by seven months, in males by nine months. In the BXSB mice, unlike either the NZ or MRL/1 animals, *males* are the more seriously afflicted (and it is believed, therefore, that the Y chromosome is somehow involved): they become ill by the age of three or four months and have a 90 percent mortality rate by eight months; females of this strain do not fall ill until the age of about one year, and there is not a 90 percent mortality rate until the age of two years.

There are also some striking differences in disease characteristics. The MRL/1 mice develop definite joint inflammation, what has been described as "lupus with superimposed rheumatoid arthritis"; they also develop monstrously swollen lymph nodes, up to one hundred times normal size. The BXSB mice's nodes swell as well, but only ten- to twenty-fold.

Both strains develop ANAs and anti-DNA antibodies, although the levels of ANAs are especially elevated in the MRL/1 mice. Antilymphocyte antibodies are also found in both strains, but at lower concentrations than in the NZ mice; they are especially low in the MRL/1 strain—and in this strain, Dr. Talal of the University of California has found, the T-cell abnormality is not a deficit of suppressor cells but unchecked proliferation of helper cells. Of the three types, *only* the MRL/1 strain harbors anti-Sm antibodies. And the oncornaviruses in both new strains apparently differ from that in the NZ mice.

The addition of these two strains has been warmly welcomed by researchers, because it is providing a much broader picture of murine (mouse) lupus—a broader range of signs and symptoms, as well as a chance to consider and investigate what may well be completely different precipitators of illness in the susceptible strains, and perhaps different genetic mechanisms that permit these precipitators to operate. The mouse picture, in brief, is now beginning to reflect the extensive variability of lupus in humans. As independent disease factors are found in the mice, that may begin to suggest similar factors in humans—and specific therapies to counter those factors, as well.

A number of therapeutic approaches have been attempted (thus far, reports have focused almost entirely on the New Zealand strains), with varying degrees of success and with varying implications for prospective human therapies.

It is clear that the thymus gland is in some way involved in the mouse disease, and that has suggested several approaches.

Dr. Talal has, for example, tried injecting bovine (cattle) thymosin into young NZB mice once a week. He found that onset of their disease was thereby delayed, but it was not prevented. And similar hormonal injections in older mice, in whom the disorder had already been established, had no effect whatever.

Dr. Alfred Steinberg of the National Institute of Arthritis, Diabetes, and Digestive and Kidney Diseases, taking a slightly different tack, has tried injecting young NZB mice biweekly with thymus cells taken from newborn normal mice. His "patients" did not become ill until their injections were discontinued at the age of one year—while an untreated control group had all developed the expected anemia by the age of four or five months. He suggests that the injected material contained suppressor T cells, possibly releasing a "censor" substance that effectively prevents inappropriate antibody production.

That something in the normal mouse thymus is missing in the model mice is evident; it is not, however, merely a matter of the abnormal thymus's producing the disorder. Thymectomy—complete removal of the thymus—has been performed on newborn mice of both strains; autoimmune disease is not prevented, and is in fact somewhat accelerated in the NZB/NZW hybrids. (If thymectomy is followed by a graft of normal newborn-mouse thymus, there is no effect one way or the other.) This acceleration of the disease process in the hybrids may suggest a partial protective role played by some component of NZW inheritance.

It appears that the spleen is a contributing factor in the disease; it is a busy center of antibody production as well as a site of erythrocyte (red-blood-cell) removal. Hence, another experimental surgical technique has been splenectomy, removal of the spleen. Results have been a bit puzzling. Young NZB mice thus treated have gone on to develop the disorder, but with less severe anemia and more severe renal disease than usual; yet, in older NZB mice, splenectomy has exacerbated the anemia and hastened death. Young NZB/NZW hybrids whose spleens are removed also become ill eventually, but their typical kidney disease is less severe than usual and they enjoy prolonged survival; the course of illness in older hybrids who are splenectomized, on the other hand, is not altered at all.

Clearly, the sex hormones have something to do with the disease in mice as they do in humans—and indeed, it has been found that female mice treated continuously with the male hormone testosterone enjoyed prolonged survival and even a normal lifespan. (No one, of course, has suggested that human females with lupus be placed on male hormones for life.) Curiously, however, the administration of danazol (Danocrine, Cyclomen), a recently developed synthetic androgen derivative, does not alter the course of the disease at all. (Danazol, essentially an antiestrogen, is used in the treatment of endometriosis, proliferation of uterine lining tissue outside the uterus, and sometimes in fibrocystic breast disease. It has a number of common side effects ranging from weight gain to acne and abnormal hair growth.)

Some of the same drugs used in treating lupus in humans (see Part Three) have also been employed in the model mice. Corticosteroids help, as they do in humans, to reduce symptoms; they also effect a modest increase in the animals' life-spans.

Immunosuppressants have also been tried. These are drugs which specifically act to suppress deleterious immune reactions, such as the rejection phenomenon in organ transplants. They also interfere with the proliferation of cells (they are used effectively in some malignancies) and for that reason are also known as cytostatics or cytotoxins ("cell killers"). And since they suppress immune reactions, they invariably lower resistance to infections, as well.

The immunosuppressant azathioprine has proved ineffective in one of the New Zealand strains and hazardous to both. While it does not influence the course of the disease in the NZB mice, it does improve the kidney-disease picture in the NZB/NZW hybrids. But in both groups its use has been associated with an alarming incidence of thymus cancer; the precise reason is not known.

The most impressive therapeutic results in the mice have occurred with the immunosuppressant cyclophosphamide, particularly in the hybrids. Given to young mice, it appears to postpone development of the disease (but not prevent it) and prolong survival. In older mice with active kidney disease, there have even been full remissions—and in some instances actual healing of lesions. But long-term administration has been associated with increased incidence of a variety of malignancies.

Another approach involves the prostaglandins, so named because they were first discovered (in the 1930s) in fluid from the prostate gland. They are by no means restricted to that site, however, and are in fact produced by all sorts of tissues throughout the body, playing active parts in many physiological processes—some such roles contradicting others. (It's possible that, as in other situations we've talked about, maintenance of health demands a balance among them.)

Based on elements of their chemical structure, the prostaglandins thus far identified fall into six groups, designated A, B, C, D, E, and F, further differentiated by subscripted numbers and suffixes. $PGE_2$ (also called dinoprostone) and

PGF$_2$-alpha (dinoprost), for example, stimulate uterine contractions and are employed to induce labor; PGE$_1$ (alprostadil) is a smooth-muscle relaxant and vasodilator. PGE$_1$ inhibits blood clotting, while PGE$_2$ promotes it. The PGAs and PGEs reduce blood pressure; the PGFs raise it. PGE$_2$ and PGF$_2$-alpha both appear to play active roles in creating inflammation (aspirin and other anti-inflammatory agents act, at least in part, by preventing their formation); PGE$_1$ reduces it, apparently by acting on B lymphocytes.

Administration of PGE$_1$ to the model mice (by subcutaneous injection) has indeed been found to greatly increase the hybrids' survival (and has also been used with some success in the MRL/1 strain). Transient side effects have included diarrhea, drowsiness, and hair loss. Further experiment, adjusting dosages, may refine the therapy and suggest potential for human use.

Total lymphoid irradiation, a technique already in experimental use in rheumatoid arthritis and discussed in Chapter 10, has been employed with heartening success in the NZB/NZW mice, greatly improving the animals' survival.

Antiviral drugs seemed to have some potential for the mice, since it has been found that virus infection exacerbates their disease, and one such drug, ribavirin, does seem to lengthen the animals' lives, probably by preventing such exacerbations rather than acting specifically against a causative agent. Unless and until an active viral agent can be demonstrated in human lupus, such drugs do not seem to hold much promise.

Two other techniques in the model mice have zeroed in on the misbehaving lymphocytes. One has involved culturing spleen cells from two-week-old hybrids or from mice of other strains, cells capable of inducing suppressor-T-cell formation, to produce a substance called soluble immune response suppressor (SIRS). Injected into sick mice three times a week, SIRS—especially that derived from an unrelated mouse strain—effected dramatic improvement, reducing autoantibody production considerably. (Transfer of T cells from healthy animals, which had occurred to researchers early on, doesn't work, because the animals quickly develop antibodies to them. In humans, there would doubtless be problems of tissue incompatibility in attempts at such treatment.)

A second technique, reported in 1983, focuses on the gene products of the mouse major histocompatibility complex, the equivalent of the human HLA region (see Chapter 5). Dr. Hugh McDevitt and his colleagues at the Stanford University School of Medicine have found that injecting antibodies to those substances—they are called *monoclonal antibodies*—can induce remission not only in murine lupus but in other autoimmune conditions (the others have been experimentally created to mimic certain other human disorders). Side effects appeared nonexistent; Dr. McDevitt was quoted as commenting that the treated mice "hopped around the cage happily." The effects also seemed to persist after treatment was stopped. The Stanford research team believes that the treatment leads to production of suppressor T cells that might move in to block the actions of either B cells or helper T cells. Whether or not this new technique will lead eventually to similar therapy for human lupus sufferers will depend on results of further animal trials.

Finally, several very *non*-high-tech tactics have been tried, consisting of various manipulations of the model animals' diets. One, depriving the mice of zinc, seemed to help but produced a number of side effects, as would such a step in humans. Zinc is a decidedly necessary trace element, and deprivation or deficiency can create a host of unpleasant problems ranging from dwarfism to delayed wound healing and severe sensory disorders, as well as nutritional imbalances leading to other ill effects.

Two other dietary manipulations which have served to help the model mice to better health and longer life seem perfectly safe. One is cutting down on total calories consumed. The other: restricting fats—which we have all been told is a good thing for other reasons, as well.

Drs. Jay Levy of the University of California and Murray Gardner of the University of Southern California have reported that NZB/NZW mice fed a high-fat diet developed

their hereditary disease almost four times faster than those
fed a low-fat diet and died long before their littermates; in
fact, only 25 percent of the low-fat-diet animals developed
disease at all. The researchers also switched some animals
from one regimen to the other; mice switched from a high- to
a low-fat diet outlived those who stayed on high fats, while
those switched from low to high fat lived shorter lives than
those who stayed on the former diet. The key mechanism:
synthesis of the inflammation-encouraging prostaglandin $E_2$
was apparently increased in the high-fat-fed animals—at
least if the same thing happened *in vivo* (in the animals) as
the scientists have observed *in vitro* (in laboratory cultures
involving fats and oils).

The researchers emphasized in their report that it made
not a whit of difference whether the fat was saturated or not.
Animals placed on high-saturated-fat (lard) diets and those on
high-unsaturated-fat (corn oil) diets fared equally poorly.

Another study, suggesting that the *kind* of fat in the diet
may be important, was reported in late 1983 by Dr. Dwight
R. Robinson of Harvard Medical School. He and his colleagues have found that fish oil—specifically, in this study,
menhaden oil—seems to have a beneficial effect in NZB/
NZW mice, retarding the progress of the renal disease that
inevitably strikes this strain and resulting in what Dr. Robinson termed "dramatic prolongation of survival." Institution
of the fish-oil-containing diet appeared not only to prevent
the development of kidney disease but even, in some cases,
to reverse it once it had begun. The Harvard researchers
hope to go on to clinical trials in humans. (The oil, which has
long been a part of the diet of some Eskimos, appears perfectly safe—and it is widely believed that the incidence of
lupus is significantly reduced among Eskimos.) They are also
pursuing further studies in the mice, testing the effects of
purified components of the fish oil, in an effort to discover
precisely what factor is responsible for the therapeutic effect.

Studies of all the mice continue and will doubtless suggest
new ways to help human lupus patients—the subject of the
final part of our book.

# PART THREE: COPING

In the first edition of this book, we commented that nonmedical friends and acquaintances, on learning that the book was in progress, were prone to reactions ranging from "Come again?" to "That's a tropical disease, right?" As we noted in Part One, lupus is a little more widely known now. These days, the response is frequently "Oh, that's the disease that killed what's-her-name."

"What's-her-name" was the gifted short-story writer and novelist Flannery O'Connor, who did indeed succumb to lupus in 1964, at the age of thirty-nine; she had first become ill in her mid-twenties. A collection of her letters, *The Habit of Being,* chronicling her life, her work, and her feelings about her illness, was published in 1980. That circumstance, perhaps, accounts for the persistent coupling of lupus with the idea of inexorable fatality—a highly inaccurate notion, nurtured until very recently by widely distributed "medical guides" employing such phrases, in describing lupus, as "usually fatal."

We would like to dispel that idea, once and for all.

A great deal has changed in the world of medicine, and statements which might have been true a generation—or even a decade—ago are not necessarily valid today. Within the authors' lifetime (and we are not yet senior citizens), there was a time when each summer brought renewed threat of epidemic polio, appendicitis was a not infrequent killer, and the treatment for pneumonia consisted of prayer and waiting for the crisis to pass.

For lupus patients, too, the outlook has changed dramatically.

When Flannery O'Connor's lupus was diagnosed in 1950, the odds were very much against her surviving another fourteen years; prior to the mid-1950s, the chance of a lupus patient's surviving *five* years was less than 40 percent. There were probably two reasons. Diagnosis thirty years ago can only be described from our present vantage point as primitive; most of the techniques in routine use today were then unheard of. Thus, when the diagnosis was finally reached *(if it was reached),* the disease was often far advanced. And therapy was, to put it mildly, a hit-or-miss affair, including drugs and other substances that were not only unhelpful but, in some cases, likely to make the situation worse.

Today, the likelihood of a lupus patient's living at least a decade are over 90 percent and rising; probably most can look forward to a normal or near-normal lifespan. We cannot go further than that speculation, for the simple reason that many of the most accurate means of diagnosis and most effective therapeutic approaches were not widely used until the 1970s, and they are still being refined and improved; patients enjoying the benefits of these advances have thus far been followed only for a dozen or fewer years.

Lupus is, in short, a *chronic* illness. That word, the dictionary will tell you, means "prolonged" or "lingering." It also means *lived with*—not "killed by."

Despite the vast progress that has been made, however, it must be said that medicine still remains at a certain disadvantage in dealing with lupus. We've alluded to most of the reasons, but it might be well to summarize them here.

*First*—and certainly foremost—the precise cause is unknown. As we have seen, many possibilities have been postulated. But none has been proved. And no present drugs known to be effective against those theoretical culprits, such as antibiotics against infectious organisms, have any effect in lupus.

*Second,* even its symptoms are unpredictable and frequently unexpected. Leaving infections aside, the manifestations of most disorders, of whatever nature, can be anticipated with a reasonable degree of confidence. And usually that means that the results of therapy and nontherapy can be anticipated as well. Severe narrowing of the coronary arteries will, if uncorrected, lead eventually to myocardial infarction. Untreated diabetes mellitus will lead to coma and death. Epilepsy uncontrolled by anticonvulsant medication will result in seizures. While the etiologies of none of these are fully understood to the last detail, the cause-and-effect pattern is clear enough to indicate specific therapy and to predict the outcome of nontreatment. Even in the various kinds of cancer, while the picture becomes more complex, therapy is directed to a specific goal and its results may be determined with some accuracy; once a focus of malignant growth has been dealt with—whether by surgery, irradiation, or drugs—the sole question is that of metastasis, spread of aberrant cells beyond the original site. (Granted, detection by current techniques is not always successful, but the object of the search is nonetheless known.)

*Third,* as we have pointed out, treatment of lupus is restricted to dealing with signs and symptoms, rather than causation. Equally necessary are shifts in therapeutic approach as those signs and symptoms abate, intensify, or change completely. The physician and patient must thus function, in lupus as in no other condition, as a partnership— analogous, perhaps, to a police team on foot patrol, never knowing from what source trouble may appear or what its nature may be (or even if it will occur at all) but constantly prepared to cope with any eventuality and ever aware that possible incidents may range from trivial to life-threatening.

*Fourth,* the course of lupus is erratic. It will not run its course like an infection, or advance inexorably like a malignancy, or pose an ever-present and unchanging threat like diabetes or another endocrine disorder. It may appear, disappear, reappear—at completely unpredictable intervals of days, months, or years—and in its reappearance may assume a wholly new and different guise.

For these reasons, lupus therapy has been and continues to

be a highly individual matter. Despite advances over the past
several decades, advances that have substantially reduced
the rates of disability and mortality, there are no hard-and-
fast guidelines and no guarantees; each patient, essentially,
presents a unique situation.

In these concluding chapters, we review the increasing,
and increasingly effective, ways in which the chronic illness
may be coped with now—including, importantly, crucial elements of self-care—and might be dealt with in the days to
come.

# 9. The Drugs: Past, Present, and—Maybe—Future

Before the late 1940s, medicine's approach to lupus was that of trial and error; looking back, it might be said that patients of that era were almost in the position of Chapter 8's experimental mice. Among the "let's try *this* and see if it works" substances employed were gold (some forms of which *are* effective in rheumatoid arthritis), bismuth, liver extracts, and an assortment of vitamins.

Since then, several types of drugs have been found effective, to varying degrees, for the multiple manifestations of lupus. None is ideal—but there is in fact no remedy for *any* condition which could be so described; in any kind of therapy, potential risks (which *all* drugs, including nonprescription products, pose) must be balanced against potential benefits. And a very great deal depends on how the drugs are used.

There is an increasing trend, now, to *conservative* treatment. That term does not refer to a political position, but to a stance in favor of administering drugs *when they are needed*. Lest it be assumed that all therapy is consistently applied in such a manner, it is, sad to say, not necessarily so among some of those involved in treating lupus over the past decade or so —a period of what can only be termed explosive growth in laboratory testing, as any patient suffering from anything at all (or perhaps nothing at all) can attest. Some have suggested that this is defensive medicine, that physicians order multitudes of tests in order to cover all bases in case of future lawsuits. That may be true in a few cases. In a probable majority, it is not; the physician simply wants to be as well informed as possible.

Laboratory testing is certainly needed in lupus; indeed, diagnosis cannot be made without it. Once that diagnosis is established, periodic reexaminations of these parameters are also called for to help assess the direction of therapy.

Lupus patients may have positive laboratory findings in the absence of active disease; in fact, as we've pointed out, some of the diagnostic facets of lupus are found in people *without* the disease. And it must be emphasized that while lab-test abnormalities may be predictors of flare-up, that is not always true. A very important report by Drs. Dafna D. Gladman, Edward C. Keystone, and Murray B. Urowitz of the University of Toronto, published in the *American Journal of Medicine* in 1979, described more than a dozen lupus patients whose lab tests were consistently abnormal but who did not really require treatment for periods varying from two to eleven years, because they simply were not sick and were functioning perfectly normally. They were thus spared the potential side effects of drug therapy. The technical term for this situation is disease that is *serologically active* but *clinically quiescent.* The Canadian physicians pointed out that "in any individual patient, it would seem advisable to determine whether the clinical course and laboratory abnormalities are concordant." (As another Canadian physician, Sir William Osler, pointed out many years ago: "It is much more important to know what sort of a patient has a disease than what sort of a disease the patient has.")

That kind of report is rare in the professional literature— with which, of course, every conscientious physician keeps up. The literature tends to focus on the comparatively complex and to raise the physician-reader's consciousness rather selectively, as Dr. John L. Decker, former chief of the Arthritis and Rheumatism Branch of the National Institute of Arthritis, Diabetes, and Digestive and Kidney Diseases points out: "The literature on the treatment of lupus tends to emphasize the emergent, severe, and active disease pattern as in-hospital events; but, of course, the vast majority of the patient's lifetime is spent at home in a state of relatively good health."* The credo of conservative therapy is: *Treat the patient, not the lab test.*

Dr. Decker goes on to underscore the importance of a continuing physician-patient relationship, so that the physician, in making treatment decisions, can take into account a spectrum of factors, including the past course of the illness and the patient's feelings, as well as current symptoms and test results. And he reminds us of the practically endless list of *other* ills lupus can mimic *and be mimicked by;* any of the symptoms of lupus we spelled out in Chapter 2 can reflect other disorders, to which lupus patients are no less subject than anyone else, rather than a flare-up of the chronic condition.

That said, let us go on to look at the medications used now in the treatment of lupus.

*Antimalarial drugs* were the first of the still-employed agents used for lupus; they have been in widespread use since shortly after World War II. There had actually been some experimental use of quinine as early as the 1890s, and similar drugs had also been reported in the 1920s as having salutary effects, particularly in clearing skin lesions. The antimalarials are not useful against kidney disease or involvement of other major organs, but can often be helpful in dealing with the skin and joint manifestations of lupus. They have been found especially useful in those patients who are photosensitive, since in addition to their anti-inflammatory action, they appear to raise the threshold of sensitivity to ultraviolet light.

The quinine derivatives—also called chloroquines—that have been most widely used in the treatment of lupus are quinacrine (Atabrine), chloroquine (Aralen), and hydroxychloroquine (Plaquenil). Side effects reported over the years

* Peter H. Schur, ed., *The Clinical Management of Systemic Lupus Erythematosus* (Grune & Stratton, 1983). Dr. Decker is now director of the Warren Grant Magnuson Clinical Center, the research hospital of the National Institutes of Health.

have been many and varied, but the most disturbing have involved the eyes.

One such effect is characterized by disturbances in vision —typically blurring when the medication is started and "halo" radiation around lights later on—due to deposits of the drug in the cornea, the transparent membrane covering the pupil at the front of the eyeball; this has been seen with all the antimalarials except quinacrine. With quinacrine, however, corneal edema (swelling due to fluid accumulation) has occurred. And corneal anesthesia may occur with any of the antimalarials; this condition, in which the ability to feel pain is deadened, could be dangerous in case of accidental injury or of overexposure to sunlight. These effects disappear after the drug has been stopped.

The second kind of eye toxicity is far more serious, because it is not reversible; even after the drug is stopped, the damage remains. It involves the retina, the area at the back of the eyeball where images are focused and from which they are relayed to the brain by the optic nerves; the damage appears to result from pigment deposits. The result is gradual restriction of vision—a narrowing of the visual field that may eventually progress to near or total blindness.

The risk of this toxic reaction is appreciably lower with quinacrine and hydroxychloroquine than with chloroquine, especially at low dosages (with quinacrine, though, a yellowish discoloration of the skin is not uncommon). Patients taking higher-than-normal doses need to be checked regularly (at least every three months) by an ophthalmologist, so that the drug can be stopped immediately if there is any hint of retinal injury. Even patients taking lower doses should have their eyes checked periodically by an ophthalmologist.

By and large, the safest antimalarial is believed to be hydroxychloroquine. It should be noted that this drug appears to be stored in fat tissues for many years. The senior author uses half the "recommended" dosage—200 milligrams every other day, instead of that amount daily—and with this regimen has never seen irreversible eye complications.

A second class of agents that can be useful in lupus is one

that goes by the name of *nonsteroidal anti-inflammatory drugs* (NSAIDs), a mouthful that simply means they act against inflammation but are not steroids (which we will come to very shortly). The most common one is aspirin, which is also an antipyretic (fever reducer) and analgesic (pain reliever) and may be the first "prescription" for fever and/or joint pain, at different dosages than those typically used for minor aches and pains. (Acetaminophen, another widely used over-the-counter analgesic—it is sold as Datril, Tempra, Tylenol, and other trade names—also reduces pain and fever but has no significant anti-inflammation action. Further, there is potential for serious kidney and liver problems from excessive use of this drug.) In cases of gastric sensitivity to plain aspirin, variations such as aspirin in buffered solution (Alka-Seltzer), time-release formulations (Cama, Measurin, et al.), or specially coated tablets (Ecotrin et al.) may be recommended.

There have also recently been introduced, specifically for treatment of rheumatoid arthritis, a number of nonsalicylate NSAIDs which have been shown to perform roughly on a par with aspirin and sometimes to result in fewer side effects—of which the major ones are tinnitus (ringing in the ears) and the gastric sensitivity previously noted—in significant numbers of patients. These prescription products include, prominently, fenoprofen (Nalfon), ibuprofen (Motrin), indomethacin (Indocin), meclofenamate (Meclomen), naproxen (Naprosyn), sulindac (Clinoril), piroxicam (Feldene), and tolmetin (Tolectin). Like aspirin, they diminish pain as well as inflammation and, like aspirin, they act to counter inflammation chiefly by inhibiting production of certain of the prostaglandins (see Chapter 8).

While these drugs have proved remarkably effective for rheumatoid arthritis and have virtually revolutionized the treatment of that condition, they have not been closely studied in relation to lupus. Further, there have been a few reports of very serious side effects, including shock and aseptic meningitis, in lupus patients given certain of these drugs—specifically, ibuprofen, sulindac, and tolmetin; these are believed due to hypersensitivity. The ARA has warned, in a recent physician advisory, that these drugs as a group tend to impair kidney function. And they also are known to complicate hypertension by promoting salt and fluid retention and by countering the action of antihypertensive medications. Thus, until more is known about these agents and their impact, they are used in lupus very cautiously, especially in patients with kidney disease or high blood pressure.

Certainly the drugs which have been found most useful in lupus are the *corticosteroids*. These are a group of agents, sometimes popularly lumped into the single word "cortisone," resembling cortisol, a hormone produced by the cortex of the human adrenal glands. There are many natural, synthetic, and semisynthetic versions and many generic names, including cortisone itself, prednisone (the most widely used in lupus), prednisolone, methylprednisolone, hydrocortisone, triamcinolone, paramethasone, betamethasone, dexamethasone, fluprednisolone, and more; there are dozens of brand names. The agents vary to a great extent in price and to a lesser extent in effects and side effects.

The corticosteroids are extremely useful drugs and are without doubt responsible for much of the dramatic improvement in the outlook for lupus patients. There is no question that they have time and again saved lives—not only in lupus but in a number of other acute conditions unresponsive to other therapies or for which no specific therapies exist. In lupus, they are administered in high doses in cases of extreme, life-threatening crisis; in low maintenance dosages on a continuing basis; and occasionally for short-term therapy of a few weeks' or months' duration.

"Low" in the foregoing sentence refers to doses of 20 milligrams or less per day, "high" to doses on the order of 40 to 200 milligrams. The medication is taken orally. Over the past few years, a new kind of corticosteroid therapy, different in both dose and route of administration, has been attempted, with success in many cases, in instances of severe deterioration in kidney function—which is, of course, a potential threat to life. This technique is referred to as "megadose" therapy (because the doses range upward from 500 milligrams), IV-MP (for "intravenous methylprednisolone"—injected methylprednisolone, the agent typically used), or "pulse therapy"; sometimes multiple injections are given at 24- or 48-hour intervals. In one of the published reports on this technique, Dr. Charles Christian and his colleagues at Cornell University Medical College noted that those who responded best had comparatively higher levels of anti-DNA antibodies as well as of immune complexes, and had had very recent deterioration of renal function.

How the corticosteroids perform is still not fully understood, but their effect, in general, is to control and suppress symptoms. They have a primary anti-inflammatory action and may inhibit the production of antibodies, as well, and it is believed they may also block the action of helper T cells (see Chapter 7). They do, at any rate, play a central role in the therapy of lupus that has failed to respond to aspirin and similar drugs (or in a patient whose sensitivity to aspirin precludes its use).

Unfortunately, there may be a number of serious side effects, which may include increased susceptibility to infection; slowed hair growth; slowed healing of injuries; hirsutism; osteoporosis (skeletal weakening due to loss of bone substance, which may heighten the risk of fractures); cataracts; masking of symptoms not only of the chronic condition but of others, such as acute infections, as well; precipitation of diabetes mellitus; aggravation of peptic ulcer (which is generally a contraindication for steroids, as is any known bacterial or fungal infection); facial swelling; elevated blood pressure and blood-lipid levels; and, occasionally, emotional problems and other highly individual reactions. (Patients who have a positive skin test for tuberculosis, indicating past infection, should also receive prophylactic anti-TB drugs if they must take corticosteroids, since the latter can otherwise reactivate the infection.)

Sometimes these difficulties, which are seen more often with continuing high dosages, can be minimized or avoided by carefully regulating dosages—i.e., keeping them as low as possible—and by administering them on an alternate-day regimen, in the morning. This approach can also lessen, but not avoid entirely, another side effect of the corticosteroids: suppression of the pituitary hormone ACTH (adrenocorticotrophic hormone), the normal function of which is stimulation of cortisol production by the adrenal glands; this occurs because there already exists a beyond-normal supply of the adrenal hormone (or a substance biochemically equivalent). Morning administration of the corticosteroid minimizes the effect, because ACTH production is highest between 4 A.M. and 8 A.M.; steroids taken in the evening can suppress it totally.

After withdrawal of long-duration corticosteroid therapy, there is an extended period of hormonal imbalance; a therapy course of eight weeks or more may mean a year of such imbalance, with a deficiency of the natural adrenal hormone. The normal function of cortisol is helping the system to withstand sudden, massive stress; it is secreted expressly in response to such stress. Therefore, during corticosteroid therapy and for at least a year thereafter, serious injury or surgery poses a distinct threat unless hormonal replacement is instituted.

The corticosteroids, in short, necessary as they are in many cases of lupus, are hardly ideal drugs. They are used only in such quantities, and for such periods, as essential, and are discontinued—by tapering, rather than by sudden cessation —as quickly as possible.

None of the systemic effects are seen with the steroid-containing creams and ointments (some available without prescription) that are used, both in lupus and in other conditions, to treat skin lesions—unless there is very extensive, prolonged application, particularly with dressings that do not permit air to reach the skin.

*Immunosuppressants* constitute another group of drugs that have been used to some degree in the treatment of lupus. They are extremely potent substances, however, and they are not without significant risk of critical side effects.

Whether they are likely to be helpful is still unclear despite a number of studies over the past few years.

Trials of these drugs stemmed initially from the fact that their function is to suppress deleterious immune reactions; they are among the agents employed to prevent "rejection" in organ transplants, a mechanism very similar to that which occurs in antigen-antibody reactions—and appears to be occurring in lupus. Further, they also interfere with the proliferation of cells (they are used effectively in some types of malignancies), and it was felt that they might attack the white cells that perpetrate some of the worst destruction in lupus. Prominent among those which have been used in lupus are azathioprine (Imuran) and cyclophosphamide (Cytoxan). Azathioprine is a cytostatic ("halting cell growth") drug, cyclophosphamide a cytotoxin ("cell poison"), and the rationale for their use is that they are inclined to attack the most rapidly proliferating cells they can find—in lupus, the antibody-producing B cells we described earlier.

A number of studies have suggested that these drugs, given in combination with prednisone, can lower the necessary dosage of the latter. In some instances, they have appeared possibly more effective than prednisone alone in staving off the recurrence of nephritis; one 1982 report termed them "of marginal benefit." (They have not been employed to treat rashes, arthritis, or other less serious manifestations of lupus.)

Many severe side effects have been documented, however, among them lowered resistance to infection; hepatitis; bone-marrow suppression (which results in anemia and deficits of other types of blood cells); sterility; and, with cyclophosphamide, severe hair loss, hemorrhagic cystitis, and malignancies including leukemias, lymphomas, and bladder cancer.

These drugs have not been approved by the Food and Drug Administration as standard lupus therapy. Because of their hazards, the initial enthusiasm for their potential has waned. As Dr. Decker of the National Institutes of Health has commented, "Given the years of intensive investigation ex-

pended on them without a clear answer, one must conclude
that their benefit:toxicity ratio is modest at best."

A new administration technique is being attempted with
cyclophosphamide—intravenous administration at monthly
intervals. It is hoped that this may minimize side effects. The
technique, which is reserved for refractory cases, thus far
appears to benefit some patients.

Two other drugs with immunosuppressant properties have
been clinically tested, but insufficient data have evolved, at
this writing, for firm conclusions. One is an anthelminthic
(drug for parasitic worm infection; it is used for roundworms)
called levamisole, which is also under study as a possible
therapeutic agent in rheumatoid arthritis. Side effects of
levamisole are few and mild. Its benefits may be few, too.
While some reports have tentatively suggested that it might
permit reduction of steroid dosages, others have found the
drug of no help at all.

The second drug, cyclosporin, is an agent that has been the
subject of glowing reports from the transplant front, where it
has turned in a remarkable performance in preventing the
rejection of grafted kidneys and other organs. While it does
not seem to affect B lymphocytes directly, it selectively inhibits the generation of helper T cells but not suppressor
T cells. Unfortunately, despite that admirable qualification,
the results of very limited clinical trials in lupus have not
been hopeful; while the drug proved effective in providing
pain relief in arthralgia, there was a high incidence of intoler-
able side effects, including nausea, vomiting, hair loss, kidney
problems, and angioedema.

Still other agents under consideration, based on extrapola-
tions from animal experiments (see Chapter 8), include
thymosin or other substances produced by the thymus
(clinical trials are already starting), inflammation-combating
prostaglandins, and monoclonal antibodies.

*Other medications* may be used from time to time in lupus,
either to prevent problems—related to the disease or to the
continuing treatment for it—or to deal with various associated symptoms. Corticosteroids, as we've mentioned, can be

associated with bone loss, and vitamin D or calcium may be prescribed. In anemia, iron may be needed. Antacids may also be suggested when a patient is taking potentially irritating anti-inflammatory medications. A variety of medications, not limited to use in lupus, may be used to cope with various conditions which may (or may not) occur in lupus patients; they may include, among others, antihypertensives, antiseizure medications, or tranquilizers.

Prompt attention to infections—which, as we've pointed out, can pose more of a risk in patients taking corticosteroids —is of course important; there are a vast number of effective antibiotics that might be used. Penicillin is generally avoided if possible (as are other agents known to cause a relatively high incidence of allergic reactions), but erythromycin is a highly effective alternative. Some of the tetracyclines are photosensitizing (and are thus avoided in patients susceptible to that phenomenon), but others are not—and again, there are usually alternatives.

Since infection is a threat, *prevention* of infection is important. A number of studies have shown that, contradictory to prior thinking, the use in lupus of the vaccines against influenza and pneumococcal pneumonia is perfectly safe (although it has been noted that a patient who is on high doses of corticosteroids may develop lower levels of antibodies in response to the vaccine and thus not enjoy as full protection). Such vaccinations are now recommended.

We noted in Chapter 3 that some 30 percent of lupus patients suffer from Raynaud's phenomenon. It is, in fact, not uncommon in young women who do *not* have lupus. The first prescription, if the patient smokes, will be immediate cessation of that habit; it is an infamous contributor to circulatory ills. In the past, not a great deal could be done beyond that, and there was resort to a variety of ploys from battery-operated hand warmers to injection of potent vasodilators, none of which worked terribly well. Fortunately, it has been found that nifedipine (Procardia), one of a new class of drugs called calcium blockers recently introduced for the treatment of coronary heart disease, also benefits those with Raynaud's; in a number of double-blind trials,† two thirds of the patients for whom the drug has been used have responded with marked improvement. Some physicians have found nifedipine effective in as many as 90 percent of patients with Raynaud's phenomenon. The only significant side effects appear to be headache, ankle edema, dizziness, and palpitations—but since it is a new agent, there may be other side effects which have not yet been recognized.

How many lupus patients may develop an unusual condition called *Sjögren's syndrome* (which, like Raynaud's, can and does occur independently) is not known, but the incidence is fairly low, certainly under 5 percent (it is much higher, at least 10 percent and possibly over 30 percent, in rheumatoid arthritis). Sjögren's is characterized by dryness due to dysfunction of various moisture-producing glands; the lacrimal (tear) and/or parotid (saliva-producing) glands are typically prominently affected. Ophthalmological testing can confirm the eye condition; special drops ("artificial tears") are used to prevent the corneal ulceration that might otherwise occur. For mouth dryness, sugarless lozenges or citrus fruits are often suggested; mouth sprays with "artificial saliva" are also available.

There are also *non*drug now and future therapies for lupus and certain of its complications; we explore these in the next chapter. And there are special considerations relating to pregnancy, to which Chapter 11 is devoted.

---

† In a double-blind trial, two "drugs" are used—the real medication being tested and an inert placebo made to look like, taste like, and in every other relevant way be indistinguishable from, the actual drug. During the trial, neither patient *nor* physician knows which substance the patient is taking; thus, the recording of reactions and results is done without bias or expectations. Only after the trial has ended are the codes assigned to the two substances broken.

# 10. Surgery and Other Options

There are a number of nondrug therapies that may be used in lupus—several employed today to handle various complications, and a couple of others that may play a part in tomorrow's treatment of the disease as a whole.

One surgical procedure that will probably be needed less in the future is sympathectomy—the severing of certain nerves contributing to Raynaud's phenomenon, in order to relieve the distressing symptoms when all else has failed. With the advent of the effective new drug treatment for this condition noted in Chapter 9, it may be hoped that the surgery can be in large part avoided.

Refractory anemia may call for special in-hospital procedures; it may require transfusion—or splenectomy, removal of the spleen. The spleen normally sequesters and destroys red blood cells that have served their purpose and are properly candidates for discard; anemia stemming from indiscriminate, premature red-blood-cell destruction can often be remedied by splenectomy. Removal of the organ, done in some other conditions as well, generally causes no ill effects, and the spleen's normal tasks are assumed by the liver and lymph nodes. The sole exception to this statement is that after splenectomy an individual is more susceptible to pneumococcal infection, and heightened alertness, with prompt antibiotic treatment should infection arise, is called for. There is also a vaccine available, and it is now recommended for lupus patients, as well as for others who have had splenectomies.

Prominent among problems that may appear to compli-

cate the lives of steroid-treated lupus patients—it may strike
up to 20 percent, according to one report from the National
Institutes of Health—is a type of bone necrosis (deterioration) variously called aseptic (non-infection-related), avascu-
lar (due to diminished blood supply), or ischemic (which
means the same thing). The problem manifests itself in joints.
Theoretically, any joint can be affected, but it is likely to be a
weight-bearing joint, and the most common site is the hip
(the bone involved is the head of the femur, the thighbone);
the second most common is the knee. The earliest symptom
of necrosis in the hip is not usually pain in the joint itself but
in the groin, the buttocks, sometimes even the knee.

If the problem persists despite conservative measures (rest
and analgesics), the solution is joint-replacement surgery,
technically termed arthroplasty. But that major surgery may
be staved off with a recently developed technique called
core decompression, which is now done even before any
abnormality is evident on X rays. This procedure, in which a
small core of tissue is taken from within the bone, was reported by Dr. Thomas M. Zizic of Johns Hopkins University,
at an ARA meeting in June 1983, to relieve pressure and
apparently to prevent an early recurrence of the problem.

Arthroplasty, which may eventually become necessary,
has made tremendous strides within the past few years. The
first joint-replacement surgery to be pronounced an unquali-
fied success was, in fact, that of the ball-and-socket joint of the
hip, based on a technique devised by the British surgeon
John Charnley. The Charnley procedure is now considered
almost routine. With more complicated hinge joints such as
the knee, technical problems have been greater—but not
insurmountable. Total knee replacement, for example, was
still considered experimental a dozen years ago; it is now the
second most common kind of arthroplasty. By 1973, strides
had been made toward designing a workable shoulder joint
(the shoulder may, uncommonly, be a necrosis site in lupus),
and that has now moved out of the experimental stage, although the operation cannot yet be called routine; the same
is true of elbow arthroplasty. Although some wrist and ankle

replacements have been performed, they are highly complex joints (there are eight separate bones in the wrist, seven in the ankle) and have posed a far greater challenge.

By far the most critical threat in lupus is kidney dysfunction. Continuing antigen-antibody-complex deposits in the glomeruli, the minuscule tufts that constitute the kidney's filtering apparatus, can progress to total necrosis (disintegration of tissues) in that vital area, with the result that waste materials remain circulating in the bloodstream. Untreated uremia, the technical term for this condition, leads inevitably to increasing physical and mental dysfunction and eventual death.

There is thus constant monitoring of kidney function of lupus patients. While the various substances in urine mentioned earlier are helpful in this regard, glomerular deterioration is not necessarily well correlated with those abnormalities. Far more specific is exploration of the creatinine-clearance rate. Creatinine is the end product of the action of creatine, a substance formed in the liver and necessary to voluntary-muscle contraction; creatinine, created by enzyme conversion in the muscle, is a waste product of that activity and is normally excreted in the urine. A high blood-creatinine level, indicative of a low clearance rate, suggests serious kidney dysfunction. BUN—blood-urea-nitrogen—elevation, while also hinting of kidney hypofunction, is less specific. Elevated BUN may be caused by renal disease, but it may occur temporarily as a result of other conditions, and test values may also be high following administration of certain drugs (which may actually raise the levels *or* may interfere with the testing itself).

One diagnostic technique is currently a topic of considerable controversy. That technique is kidney biopsy—removal of a small amount of kidney tissue for microscopic examination. Some researchers argue that the precise nature of the nephritis (kidney inflammation) must be known in order to guide treatment, and that the procedure should be performed on all patients whenever there are urinary abnormalities. Many other physicians feel, however, that it is unnecessary to subject a patient to renal biopsy except under very limited conditions. One of these is a suspicion of renal vein thrombosis, blockage by clotting, since this condition may require prompt administration of anticoagulants or even surgical intervention; such a possibility is of particular concern when there has been a sudden deterioration in renal function.

Development of kidney dysfunction, while occasionally rapid, more typically takes place gradually over a period of months or years, and in most cases does not progress to a critical stage; many lupus patients continue to function quite well with varying degrees of renal insufficiency. But if kidney deterioration does reach that life-threatening stage and fails to respond to medication, there are only two alternatives. They are hemodialysis—periodically filtering the patient's blood through a mechanical device, an "external kidney," that performs the purification—or kidney transplant.

The unfortunate—and inaccurate—medical term for this point in the course of lupus has been "end stage" renal disease, a term which is beginning to appear in quotes in titles of medical-journal articles. It certainly is not a stage, as it might have been thirty years ago, suggesting that death is near. It has now been realized that it does not even necessarily denote the demise of spontaneous kidney function; seemingly final renal failure may sometimes be strictly temporary. By early 1983, a number of published reports had suggested that recovery of renal function might occur in close to 30 percent of patients. Later that year, Drs. Robert P. Kimberly and Michael D. Lockshin and their colleagues published the results of a study of all lupus patients who had undergone dialysis at New York Hospital–Cornell Medical Center over a twelve-year period, from January 1, 1970, to January 1, 1982 (a few patients whose prior histories lacked significant data and who had been specifically referred to the center for dialysis were excluded). Over 40 percent recovered renal function and were able to discontinue dialysis.

It has been three decades since the first completely successful kidney transplant was performed in 1954, between identical twins, at Peter Bent Brigham Hospital in Boston. During the dozen years after that, nearly half the attempted grafts failed. But two technological advances have combined to vastly improve the transplant track record: sophisticated histocompatibility matching between donors and recipients (see Chapter 5 for more on the subject) and the development of ways to keep a kidney viable for many hours and over many miles (international organ shuttles are now routine).

So common had kidney transplants become by 1977 that in that year, the International Human Renal Transplant Registry stopped keeping tabs on them. In its final report, which put the world total then at close to 25,000, it estimated the five-year graft survival rates at 78 percent for sibling kidneys, almost 75 percent for parent-to-child grafts, and over 50 percent for kidneys from unrelated donors. Rates at the more experienced transplant centers have exceeded these figures, and the success rates in lupus patients are no lower than those in others. *(Graft* survival does not mean the same as *patient* survival; when a transplanted kidney fails or is rejected, another transplant can be attempted.)

Finally, two new procedures are now under intensive study for their potential in treating rheumatoid arthritis and possibly lupus as well.

One, called apheresis, is based on a principle similar to that of dialysis. In the latter, the patient's blood is circulated outside the body to flush out waste materials that would normally be eliminated by the kidneys. What if circulating antibodies, immune complexes, and other troublemakers could be flushed out periodically by a similar process?

The process is variously called plasmapheresis, lymphapheresis, or lymphoplasmapheresis, depending upon whether plasma, lymphocytes, or both are filtered out; most of the experience has been with plasmapheresis. In rheumatoid arthritis, it has been found to provide some relief from pain and disability, although the effect has been short-lived.

So far as lupus goes, the technique is in its infancy—and any applications of it at this point are strictly experimental. The results of the trials thus far have been, to put it mildly, mixed, varying from lengthy remissions in a few patients to brief remissions to no improvement whatever, and a disturbing factor is that in a number of the preliminary reports, sustained remissions have occurred only when the procedure was followed by administration of the hazardous immunosuppressant cyclophosphamide.

Other drawbacks include expense—plasmapheresis could cost an individual patient several hundred thousand dollars a year—and the delicate nature of the procedure; as Dr. Daniel J. Wallace, who heads a research team at Cedars-Sinai Medical Center in Los Angeles, has warned, "If patients are not properly monitored and the procedure is not performed with great care, life-threatening complications could arise." In any case, a five-year study, involving sixteen medical centers and supported by the National Institute of Arthritis, Diabetes, and Digestive and Kidney Diseases, began in 1982, and the results should resolve some of the questions. It has also been noted that the technology in this area is comparatively primitive and that further refinements—perhaps filtering out only B cells, or helper T cells, or particular antibodies—may eventually prove both feasible and of greater benefit.

The second experimental treatment is known as total lymphoid irradiation (TLI), in which radiation is carefully beamed to lymph nodes and other tissues where lymphocytes congregate. TLI has been used for some two decades in treating Hodgkin's disease and other forms of lymphoma (malignancies involving the lymph system), and the treatment has been found both safe and effective in those conditions.

Experience with TLI in autoimmune disease is far more limited. Results to date in rheumatoid arthritis and lupus patients—the major studies have been taking place at Stanford University Medical Center and at Harvard—have been promising, with the majority of patients improving, and reported side effects have been minimal. The treatment appears to work by decreasing the proportion of helper cells in the patients' T-cell population.

# 11. Conception and Contraception

We noted earlier that pregnancies in lupus patients have evidenced higher-than-average rates of both spontaneous abortion and premature births, and that there has been a significant incidence of disease flare-ups both early in pregnancy and later, in the postpartum period, when production of progesterone (which is produced in high quantities by the placenta) falls off. Because of these risks, it was once thought wise for all lupus patients to avoid pregnancy, since it seemed impossible to predict whether or not trouble was in store for mother, fetus, or both.

With more careful studies and correlation of certain maternal characteristics with pregnancy outcomes, it appears that pregnancy is not as broadly hazardous in lupus as it seemed. Pregnancy is still considered unwise if there is seriously impaired function of the kidneys or of any other major organ or organ system, or if there was a severe flare-up of disease during a prior pregnancy (suggesting that the same thing is likely to happen again). Beyond that, it has been found that problems in pregnancy—including complications of pregnancy, flare-up of lupus, and untoward effects on the fetus— are significantly correlated with the mother's condition at the time of conception *and for the six months prior to conception:* complete remission for at least that long is statistically associated with uncomplicated full-term pregnancy (although there is no guarantee), while active disease at the time of conception is associated with the highest incidence of the mother's condition worsening and of miscarriage, stillbirth, or premature birth. There is *no* correlation with the length of time since diagnosis—and as we previously noted, lupus may in fact be first diagnosed following pregnancy.

There have been few studies linking specific serological findings with pregnancy outcomes; those which have been reported tentatively suggest an association with miscarriage of both ANAs and anti-Ro antibodies. It may be that further studies along these lines will point to other factors that may prove predictive of the outcome of pregnancy in lupus patients.

The threat to the fetus is probably due to placental passage of antibodies and may be due to impact on the placenta itself. In one study reported in 1980, Dr. Carlos R. Abramowsky and his colleagues at Case Western Reserve University examined the placentas from a group of lupus patients. Half the pregnancies had culminated in live births, and no abnormalities were found in the placentas. Of the others, which were associated with miscarriage or stillbirth, vascular lesions were found in 80 percent.

We have stated that lupus is not directly inherited. There has been a very small incidence, among babies born to lupus patients, of something called for want of a better term "neonatal (newborn) lupus," which appears to be associated, again, with transplacental—especially anti-Ro—antibodies; one 1983 study also reported a significant association with HLA-DR3 in the mothers (see Chapter 5). This condition is typically manifested by transient cutaneous symptoms and/ or congenital heart block—not a complete halt (as it may sound to the lay person) but a medical term for misfiring of certain electrical signals within the heart which results in irregularities of the heartbeat, occasionally serious enough to require a pacemaker; in a small percentage, blood-cell abnormalities are also found. In most of these babies, the condition resolves spontaneously by the age of six months to one year, and the antibodies disappear from the babies' bloodstreams, as well.

There is no evidence, incidentally, that continued treatment of lupus during pregnancy with such drugs as corticosteroids has any adverse effect on the fetus. In fact, with a view to countering the stress of labor and preventing post-partum exacerbation, many physicians now feel it advisable to increase the dosage of such drugs about the time of delivery and to continue it for three to eight weeks, tapering it gradually thereafter. There is general agreement that antimalarial drugs should not be used during pregnancy. There is also general agreement that, except in special circumstances, aspirin and other nonsteroidal anti-inflammatory drugs should not be used, since they may cause serious problems, especially hypertension. And while immunosuppressants have not been found to have immediate fetal or newborn impact, they *may* cause genetic or other injury, the results of which would not appear for many years; hence, they are also avoided.

What about drugs taken by the nursing mother? It is known that *most* medications do slip into breast milk to some degree, but little research has been done on this question specifically relating to lupus patients. Dr. Peter H. Schur of Harvard Medical School, who is also director of the Clinical Immunology Laboratory and Lupus Clinic at Brigham and Women's Hospital in Boston, has made the helpful suggestion that medications be taken just after breast feeding, on the theory that they will be mostly absorbed and metabolized before the next feeding and the amount that might enter the mother's milk will be minimized.

For the lupus patient who, because of potential complications or simply personal choice, wishes to avoid pregnancy: There is a clear consensus that oral contraceptives, which are combinations of estrogens and one form or another of progestin, a synthetic form of progesterone, are best avoided. In women in general who take one form or another of "the pill," there is evidence of an increased risk of such circulatory problems as high blood pressure, vasculitis (blood-vessel inflammation), and thrombosis; since lupus patients are already at higher-than-average risk so far as these conditions are concerned, it does not seem sensible to further raise those odds. Intrauterine devices (IUDs) pose in all women some risk of perforation, bleeding, or pelvic infection; that risk rises, for reasons that are not fully understood, to a perilous 50 percent in lupus.

Thus, barrier contraceptives—the diaphragm with spermicidal jelly, the condom, the sponge, or the cervical cap—are the devices of choice. It should be added that while the statistical track records of these methods are somewhat lower than that of oral contraceptives, many knowledgeable observers have pointed out that the published figures include numerous cases of misuse (i.e., failing to follow instructions) and disuse (failing to use at all). There are also other alternatives on the horizon, including, possibly, the long-awaited "male pill."

## 12. Sun, Sex, Stress, and Other Dilemmas: A Special Message for Patients

This chapter offers some additional facts, some practical advice, and some hopefully helpful suggestions. It is based neither on intensive research nor on broad surveys but in great part on the senior author's own experience in treating patients and in lesser but significant part on letters from readers of the first edition of this book. Those readers sought both solid information and help for a host of unexpected difficulties.

We want to start with a reminder that if you have lupus, you do not have a "fatal disease." You have a *chronic* disease, like diabetes, or rheumatoid arthritis, or any of a number of other disorders that make life less comfortable and more complicated for a great many people. There are many things that you can do to make your own life easier and less burdensome, however, both physically and emotionally.

Before we come to those, a brief note about physicians. Many of the letters we have received are from patients who do not know where to turn for authoritative medical advice —or who question the medical advice they have received. Some of the latter, we must add, have been absolutely right to do so. As one bewildered woman wrote us after delineating symptoms and laboratory tests that certainly should have aroused a high index of suspicion of lupus, "Dr. A. stated emphatically before even taking my history that I did not have lupus because I lacked the butterfly rash, which he

explained all lupus patients had." That is, of course, completely untrue.

Your first recourse, in seeking a specialist, should be the
physician who cares for you regularly—your internist, gyne-
cologist, or family physician. That doctor is a good start for
referral because he or she knows you well and, if there is a
choice among specialists, will make some effort to pair you
with one with whom you will feel comfortable.

If you don't have a regular doctor—or you are in the position of our correspondent (or you're just unhappy with your
present physician)—your best recourse is a call to the nearest
medical school or teaching hospital, a medical center affiliated with a medical school. Ask for the department of medicine; the person you want is a specialist in rheumatology,
which is a subspecialty of internal medicine. You may be
referred to a staff physician, or to a rheumatologist in private
practice who is affiliated with the medical center; such a
physician generally contributes a certain amount of time to
teaching students and residents (medical-school graduates
who are receiving further training in the various specialties).

We may as well mention the matter of board certification.
Specialists are not compelled by law to prove themselves
knowledgeable in a particular area of medicine in order to
practice, or even to term themselves specialists. All practicing physicians must, of course, pass licensing examinations.
Some choose to go further and subject themselves to special
written and oral examinations given by boards of acknowl-
edged experts; the physicians who pass these examinations
are called *board-certified* or "boarded," or *diplomates* of the
particular board. (A certain amount of actual experience is a
prerequisite; a physician who has had that experience but has
not yet taken the exams is said to be *board-eligible.*) This is
not to say that there are not many competent and caring
physicians who are not board-certified; there are. But board
certification—in rheumatology, this means certification in internal medicine followed by certification in the subspecialty
—does attest, at least, to an objectively established competence.

Most physicians display licenses and board certifications in their offices. Some do not. It is wholly within the patient's rights to ask to see these documents.

Now—how can you, as a lupus patient, help yourself?

We said earlier that the physician and patient must function as a team; in perhaps no other disorder is the patient's part of that teamwork so vital. Constant preoccupation with one's ills is not particularly desirable. Still, a continual awareness is important. Unfamiliar symptoms should be promptly reported to your doctor—and *don't* automatically assume that everything is a symptom of lupus, despite the broad spectrum of manifestations we've described. An unexpected development could signal lupus activity. It could also mean an untoward reaction to a medication. And it could possibly mean something entirely different.

Speaking of medications, we want to emphasize something that really applies to anyone with any condition who is under medical treatment but especially applies in lupus, both because of the unpredictable nature of the disease and because of the potent drugs that must be used to treat it. *Don't* take any *other* drugs on your own, without consulting your physician. This applies not only to something that may be prescribed by another doctor (put them in touch with each other) but to over-the-counter drugs as well, even those as presumably innocent as antacids and minor pain relievers. Some such drugs could worsen your illness (many antacids, for instance, have sodium levels hazardous to those with hypertension). Others could interact dangerously with drugs your physician has prescribed—or counteract, and diminish the beneficial effects of, the latter.

You should also check with the doctor who is treating your lupus before you have any dental work done, as well as any examination in which there is the slightest chance of injury, including sigmoidoscopy (examination of the lower intestine) and standard gynecological procedures. The reason is prevention of problems. There is a small but significant incidence in lupus of a condition called Libman-Sachs endocarditis, in which there are tiny growths on the heart valves.

Typically, they do not cause any serious problems—*except* if they become infected, resulting in a condition called sub-acute bacterial endocarditis, which is damaging but extremely difficult to detect. Many physicians feel it's best to forestall that possibility by giving prophylactic antibiotics. (The antibiotic of choice varies with the type of procedure and may be given orally or by injection; it is typically administered thirty to sixty minutes before the procedure and repeated a specified number of hours afterward.)

Another protective step you can take is to avoid both known and possible triggers of trouble. That includes a variety of elements from weather to chemicals found in everyday products.

Extreme cold can be an exacerbating element for some lupus patients, and if you have found you are one of those, you should take appropriate care in winter weather; for a few patients, extreme heat may have similar effects. A significant number of lupus patients—at least one third—are extremely sensitive to the sun, which may trigger not only skin lesions but arthritic symptoms and a variety of systemic problems, as well. If you are among them, take precautions to avoid over-exposure, including protective clothing (even if a limited area is exposed, such as an arm in an open car window while driving), avoidance of sunlight during the midday hours, and awareness of deceptive refracted- and reflected-light situations that can increase exposure; sand, snow, water, glass, even sidewalks can reflect light in apparent shade—and light can also be intensified by refraction through atmospheric haze and the water of lakes or pools. Effective sunscreens should be used whenever lengthy exposure to the sun is unavoidable.

Effective *physical* sunscreens are opaque creams, generally containing a substance such as zinc oxide, that block the sun's rays completely. *Chemical* sunscreens filter out the most harmful of those rays; among the most effective active ingredients are PABA (para-aminobenzoic acid) and padimate. Sunscreens are now rated in the United States, as they had been in Europe for some time, with a number called a sun protection factor (SPF). SPFs range generally from 2 to 15, with a few ranging up to 18; the higher the number, the greater the protection. If you're photosensitive, your sunscreen should have the highest SPF you can find. And in case you find yourself envying friends their glowing tans, know that while their basking may not create any present problems for them, they are asking for future trouble: sun exposure is without question related both to premature aging and to the development in later years of skin cancer.

It appears, too, that allergies occur significantly more often among lupus patients than among people in general, and for that reason it is probably wise to avoid substances widely known to act as provoking allergens in those who are sensitive to them. Permanent hair colorings are among these substances (the warning does not apply to water-soluble temporary rinses or to simple lighteners), as are many ordinary cosmetics. We would suggest relying for lipstick, eye makeup, etc., on one of the several reputable lines of hypoallergenic cosmetics, from which the pigments and other elements most likely to act as allergens have been excluded.

There is no absolute proof that drugs known to trigger a reversible lupuslike illness, which we mentioned in Chapter 2, are related to exacerbations of lupus itself; some of these drugs have in fact been used in lupus patients without demonstrable ill effect. On the other hand, there is not absolute evidence that they never exacerbate the disease, either, and it is probably wise to avoid them if possible. It has now been reported that hydrazine, a chemical fraction of one of those drugs, hydralazine, can induce lupuslike disease; the phenomenon was reported in a laboratory technician who had been exposed to the chemical in her work, simply by its touching her skin. There was complete correlation between remission and removal of the substance from her environment, and between recurrence and subsequent reexposure (done deliberately, under medically supervised challenge).

This is by way of noting that hydrazine and its derivatives are found in a number of food and other products. Some of these are virtually unavoidable in the course of daily life. But we think it sensible to avoid those with which encounters are unnecessary, including herbicides, pesticides, photographic supplies, and dyes—as well as tobacco and mushrooms, in which hydrazine occurs naturally. A chemical cousin of hydrazine, called tartrazine, occurs in the form of an FDA-approved coloring called FD&C Yellow #5, found in many cosmetics and food products ranging from hair rinses and bath salts to prepared breakfast cereals and some soft drinks. The putative troublemakers in the other major lupus-inducing drug, aromatic amines, also occur as breakdown products of some food dyes, as well as in permanent hair colorings—and can be absorbed through the skin. So far as foods go, we think what makes a good deal of sense not only for lupus patients but for everyone is a balanced diet based as little as possible on processed foods (most of which contain more salt than is necessary or desirable for anyone).

Lest it be thought we are advocating the products generally purveyed at "health food" stores, we are not; the ingredients of a healthful diet can be found at any supermarket. In fact, we especially warn against the variety of "herbal" products sold in the former establishments, some of which have been found distinctly unhealthful and have precipitated critical allergic reactions and worse. A "naturally grown food" is not necessarily harmless.

We might, in this regard, mention the case of Dr. Malinow's macaques. Dr. M. Rene Malinow and his colleagues at the Oregon Regional Primate Research Center had been testing alfalfa seeds in monkeys and rabbits as a potential agent for lowering cholesterol; he also took some himself to see what effect it might have in humans. His cholesterol level dropped; he also developed anemia, other blood-cell abnormalities, and ANAs.

An experiment was set up in which ten female macaques were fed a nourishing diet, with five receiving alfalfa seeds in addition. The five control monkeys thrived. Three of the five who were fed the alfalfa seeds became ill with symptoms that included facial rash, hair loss, hemolytic anemia, high ANA levels, and what were described as "remarkable" amounts of anti-DNA antibodies; one soon died of infection. The other two survived, although they remained ill until they were treated with a short course of corticosteroids.

That's *induction,* of course, *not* exacerbation of *existing* lupus. But in 1983, Drs. Jimmy L. Roberts and James A. Hayashi of Rush Medical College in Chicago reported two cases of lupus patients who had had flare-ups after they had enjoyed fairly lengthy remissions while maintained on low doses of prednisone. Both flare-ups followed the patients' admitted consumption of alfalfa tablets.

Then, there is the matter of stress. A number of chronic ills seem, for unknown reasons, to be subject to exacerbation by stress of various types, both physical and emotional; among them are epilepsy, peptic ulcers, migraine, heart disease, some gum disorders, hypertension, and asthma and a number of other allergic conditions. Lupus shares this susceptibility in general, with a couple of additional exacerbating factors.

Stress, of course, can't always be avoided. But some kinds of stress can, to a degree. Physical stresses include infection, injuries, and undue fatigue, all of which can produce lupus flare-ups and all of which can to some extent be avoided. Don't knowingly expose yourself to contagious ills, major or minor. Take safety rules seriously (everyone should, of course). Don't drive yourself to the point of utter fatigue; take rest periods during the day if you need them, and get a full night's sleep. Maintain your general health by the balanced diet we mentioned earlier—including weight loss under your doctor's supervision if that seems desirable, and, during periods of remission, a program of regular exercise (bearing in mind the safety precautions we've noted; by far the safest exercise is swimming, and professional physical therapy can also be helpful when arthritis is a problem).

Lupus can also be emotionally stressful, and there may be a vicious cycle at work. The symptoms themselves can create a good deal of anxiety, depression, or both; no one likes to feel rotten, and a lupus flare-up can make one feel very, very rotten. And prednisone and related drugs, especially in the

dosages needed to control serious disease activity, can themselves cause emotional changes. Further, stress—which may
stem from either of these—perhaps can itself trigger flare-
ups; we're not sure, but many physicians and patients agree
that it's likely.

Happily, in many cases that cycle can be broken, and we'll
address ourselves to that shortly. First, we'd like to deal with
a very special area, one which is a critical concern to many if
not most patients, although it is discussed far less than it
should be, both in the doctor's office and in print. That area is
sexual relations. It's vital for a patient and her (or his) partner
to realize that both problems that are part of lupus *and* the
drugs used to treat those problems may from time to time
cause sexual difficulties. We think the important thing is for
couples to be aware of these possibilities, so that there are no
misinterpretations—and to be aware, as well, that there are
ways in which these difficulties can be dealt with.

Let's take, first, some of the medications that may be used.
Tranquilizers have been known, for example, to interfere
with orgasm; knowledge of this fact may, we hope, allay some
"What did I do wrong?" worries. Antihypertensives not infrequently cause erectile dysfunction in men—*not* necessarily, it must be stressed, orgasmic dysfunction (the two are
controlled by different sets of nerves); when this occurs, a
couple may find gratification by other means than the traditional.

The corticosteroids may cause a number of sexually perti-
nent problems. They may, for one thing, decrease libido or
sexual desire—and the partner should not conclude that he
(or she) is being summarily rejected personally; a little more
effort may be required to overcome this diminished desire.
Second, there is the possibility of missed menstrual periods—
which normally may signal pregnancy, but that is not necessarily so if a woman is taking these medications. A third
problem is easy skin bruisability; "Ouch!" should be heard
literally, not as "Don't touch me." Fourth, a potential compli-
cation of steroid therapy is, as we've mentioned, necrosis of
bone particularly affecting the hip joint; it can be extremely

painful and can definitely interfere with your comfortably positioning yourself for sexual intercourse.

There are also a number of manifestations of lupus itself that can pose problems in sexual relations. If you are one of the minority of women with lupus—probably fewer than one in twenty—who suffer from vaginal ulcers (a variant of the mouth and throat sores we listed in Chapter 3 among the diagnostic criteria), you know that they can mean painful sexual intercourse. They *will go away;* in the meantime, it will help to explore other routes to sexual gratification (open minds are distinct assets). On the other hand, mouth ulcers may occur, which can make oral contacts painful; they, too, disappear eventually.

Another difficulty may be posed by a variant of Sjögren's syndrome, in which there is a drying of the tear glands or the salivary glands, as we mentioned in Chapter 9; sometimes, this drying-of-normal-secretions phenomenon may affect the lubricating glands which normally ease entrance of the penis into the vagina. The result is very painful intercourse. The solution is a lubricant—a water-soluble type such as KY, since such agents as petroleum jelly can be absorbed and cause circulatory complications—or, again, a possible change of habits.

Raynaud's phenomenon, as we noted earlier, afflicts some 30 percent of lupus patients, causing pain in the fingers and/ or toes. That pain can increase during sexual activity, simply because blood flow is diverted to the genital area; that is, the situation is intensified. Your partner should be made aware that pressure on the affected area can increase the discomfort. It may also help to precede sexual relations with a warm bath and to be sure that the room is adequately heated.

Joint pain, of course, can put a significant crimp in range and ease of movement in sexual activities as it can elsewhere. Here, some individual experimentation is often helpful, and the guideline is: What works for the particular couple? If there is knee pain, for instance, avoid flexion and choose positions that put no burden of weight on the knees. If one hip or knee is affected, a lateral (on-the-side) position with that joint upward can be helpful—as can a short-term "anesthetic" in the form of a just-before cold pack. If both knees are involved, avoid intertwining legs, since that is likely to cause increased pain. And if there is all-over achiness, think about the fact that sexual gratification can be achieved strictly by oral or manual activity.

Perhaps it's obvious, but we'll say it anyway. All that we have been discussing, the attainment (or reattainment) of good and satisfying relations between the lupus patient and her (or his) sexual partner, demands one vital factor at the start: complete honesty and frankness between the partners. The patient should not play martyr, but should fully explain feelings and discomforts, pains and pleasures—and insecurities, too. The partner (who, we hope, will have read the preceding chapters and so gained an understanding of the illness itself) must develop understanding and sympathy, adapt to the afflicted partner's limitations—and, above all, actively cooperate in seeking solutions that will be satisfying to both.

Many a physician can affirm that often, when food restrictions have been imposed upon a patient, the exercise of creative imagination has actually resulted in the new diet's being more interesting and enjoyable than the old. That can apply, and has applied, in the area of sexual relations as well.

To return to the general question of stress: we suggested that the cycle could be broken. The active intervention, beyond the basics we've talked about thus far, is in the emotional area; it may take a variety of forms.

Sometimes, the problem appears suddenly and is perceived first by someone other than the patient. As the mother of a fifteen-year-old wrote us, "My daughter has recently been diagnosed as having lupus. She was hospitalized and is now home, taking prednisone. This has come on us very suddenly. Her emotions and temperament have changed, and we are having a hard time handling this."

Another letter, we think, summarized the emotional problems very articulately and also strongly suggested part of the solution. Our correspondent said some nice words about the first edition of this book and continued, "I read it at a very critical time in my life—when I was just beginning to truly accept my disease, about four years after the diagnosis. Sometimes it takes that long! It was also very meaningful to my family. . . . I am [in my early thirties and a mother]. I would consider my marriage to be a very sound and strong one. However, my husband and I have our periods of hell because of lupus, and we find that it requires constant working-out and deep communication all along the way."

We think that vicious stress cycle can be broken in three ways, not necessarily independent of one another.

One is a way we suggested to the mother of the fifteen-year-old: psychotherapeutic counseling. It is not an admission of total ineptitude to declare, to yourself and to your doctor, that you are having trouble coping with an illness that has markedly disrupted your life. Such counseling, depending upon your individual situation, may take the form of individual therapy, sex or marital counseling, family therapy, or a combination thereof. Your physician should be able to recommend a qualified individual, who may be a psychiatrist, a psychologist, or a social worker.

Second: our last-quoted correspondent made two points we think are highly significant. One is that the acceptance of the diagnosis of a chronic illness is often difficult, and understandably so: it may indeed take weeks, months, or even years before you—and your family—can say to yourselves, "This is a continuing problem that we are going to live with from now on, and we are going to have to adjust our lives to it." The second is, as she put it, "deep communication." Of course, this concept applies to any situation affecting marital and/or family relations; "communicate" is probably the most repeated word in the many magazine articles that deal, often vapidly and repetitively, with family relationships. But its overuse does not invalidate it. Communication—which means *honest* communication—is indeed essential. That entails making your feelings known about the situation *and* listening openly to others' feelings. If you care about one another, there will be some movement in the direction of accommodation and adjustment.

Communication also involves understanding of the *facts* of any situation, and we were delighted that our correspondent mentioned that our book had proved meaningful not only to her but to others in her family. If you are a lupus patient reading this book, we hope you will share it with the person or persons closest to you. That may well dispel a great deal of misunderstanding.

Finally, we want to applaud and endorse the proliferation of self-help or support groups. Sometimes it is helpful simply to share problems with others who have similar concerns. It tells you, at the very least, that you are not alone; at best, you will be offered solutions to those problems by those who have encountered them before you. With half a million to one million lupus patients in our nation, you are most assuredly not alone.

Sometimes such groups consist simply of patients who gather together on their own to exchange information and confide in one another. Often they meet under the leadership or guidance of a physician, social worker, psychologist, or other experienced counselor.

The Lupus Foundation of America is a national self-help group, with local chapters in many areas, which has funded major research and maintains a cross-country informational network. It publishes a quarterly newsletter, *Lupus News,* as well as booklets on special aspects of coping with the disease, such as securing Social Security disability status and dealing with child care. Check your phone book under "lupus" or contact the Foundation's headquarters: 11673 Holly Springs Drive, St. Louis, MO 63141; (314) 872-9036.

The Arthritis Foundation, which funds research in, and has available literature on, all the rheumatic disorders including lupus, also offers advice on forming such groups and has branches in most areas. The national headquarters is at 1314 Spring Street NW, Atlanta, GA 30309.

And for additional literature, especially as relating to the latest research and statistical data, you can write the government agency under whose umbrella lupus falls: National Institute of Arthritis, Diabetes, and Digestive and Kidney Diseases, Bethesda, MD 20505.

# INDEX

# ABOUT THE AUTHORS

*Sheldon Paul Blau, M.D.*, is director of the Division of Rheumatic Diseases at Nassau County Medical Center (New York State) and clinical professor of medicine at the School of Medicine, State University of New York at Stony Brook. A Fellow of the American College of Physicians, he is a diplomate of the American Board of Internal Medicine both in that specialty and in the subspecialty of rheumatology. Dr. Blau serves as chairman of the Medical and Scientific Advisory Committee of the Long Island division of the Arthritis Foundation and as a member of its board of trustees; he is also chairman of the Medical Advisory Board of the Lupus Erythematosus Foundation of Long Island and a member of the Medical Advisory Board of the Scleroderma Society of Greater New York. Dr. Blau is editor and co-author of the medical texts *Rheumatoid Emergencies* and *Review Book in Internal Medicine.*

*Dodi Schultz* is an award-winning science writer who collaborated with Dr. Blau on the first edition of this book as well as on a prior work on arthritis; she is also author or co-author of more than a dozen other books, and her articles appear frequently in the leading magazines. Ms. Schultz is a member of the Authors Guild and serves on the board of directors of the American Society of Journalists and Authors.